MEN-AT-ARMS SERIES

EDITOR : MARTIN WINDROW

Napoleon's Line Chasseurs

Text by EMIR BUKHARI

Colour plates by ANGUS McBRIDE

OSPREY PUBLISHING LONDON

Published in 1977 by
Osprey Publishing Ltd,
12–14 Long Acre, London WC2E 9LP
Member company of the George Philip Group

ISBN 0 85045 269 4

The author would like to express his gratitude for the
assistance rendered him by the following persons in the
preparation of this book: the members of the staff of
the Musée de l'Armée, Paris, and the National Army
Museum, London; Jean de Gerlache de Gomery;
Sharon Massey; Blaise Morgan; Richard Hook and
Maximilian Luchese. Finally and most particularly to
M. Lucien Rousselot whose work on the French Army
serves as model and inspiration to all writers and
illustrators seeking to spread knowledge of the
uniforms of this period. The majority of the line
drawings in this book were prepared from his faultless
renderings.

Filmset by BAS Printers Limited Wallop, Hampshire
Printed in Hong Kong

Organisation

By 1793 the number of light cavalry regiments of the French army had more than doubled their total of 1789, while the number of medium and heavy regiments had increased by a paltry four. The fact that the *chasseurs à cheval* regiments should now number twenty-six against a bare twelve, four years previously, is highly indicative of the state of the army as a whole; the role of light cavalry involved reconnaissance and the screening of the main army, leaving the body blows to the more professional heavy cavalry, and they were thus far more easily raised and trained. The chasseurs, being the indigenous French light horse, can perhaps therefore be equated best with the infantry *demi-brigades* of this period, a half-trained, unprofessional, make-shift collection, making up with zeal what they lacked in experience.

By the turn of the Empire, the chasseurs numbered twenty-four regiments, listed 1 through 26 with the 17th and 18th being vacant. Five further regiments were created during the course of the wars:

The 27th Chasseurs, formed 29 May 1808 from the Belgian *Chevau-Légers d'Arenberg*.

The 28th Chasseurs, created on the same date from Tuscan dragoons originally organised in January 1808.

The 29th Chasseurs formed late in 1810 from the *3eme Régiment Provisoire de Cavalerie Légère* raised in Spain in 1808.

The 30th Chasseurs, formed by an Imperial decree of 3 February 1811, were chasseurs on paper only, as they were promptly converted to *Chevau-Légers Lanciers*.

The 31st Chasseurs raised 7 September 1811 from the amalgamation of the *1er and 2eme Régiments Provisoires de Cavalerie Légère*.

Chasseurs regiments were composed of between four and six squadrons. A squadron comprised two companies of two troops and was commanded by an *adjutant*. Companies were commanded by *capitaines* and troops by *lieutenants* or *sous-lieutenants*. The regimental chain of command was identical to that of the heavy cavalry, and readers are referred to the author's previous title in this series, *Napoleon's Cuirassiers and Carabiniers*.

1. **Chef d'escadron in full dress, 1800. In near hussar dress,** *mirliton* **cap, dolman, barrel-sash, Hungarian breeches and boots, this superior officer based on a painting by Hoffman serves to illustrate the origins of chasseur uniform against which hussar-based influence it continually strove throughout the Empire, terminating in an individual chasseur style all its own. (Huen. Courtesy NAM)**

3

2. Officers, 1800. They wear the 1806-pattern shako, recognized officially at that date despite having been worn under the Consulate, and the 1791-model chasseur *caracot*, similar though longer than the hussar dolman, beneath which we can see the heavily braided, sleeveless waistcoat. Though both wear sabretaches, these became an increasingly rare sight during the Napoleonic Wars. The shako cords, soon to become obsolete, at this period served to secure the headgear when riding. (Benigni. Courtesy NAM)

Dress and Equipment

At the beginning of the Consulate, chasseurs' dress was essentially that prescribed by the decree of 1 April 1791. By 1795 the *mirliton* hussar-cap had universally replaced the fur-crested Tarleton-style helmet. The dolman tunic was still worn, though, as we shall see, it was soon to be replaced by the familiar *habit-long*; this in turn was to be superseded by a short-tailed, single-breasted 'Kinski' tunic, predecessor to the *habit-veste* of 1812 pattern. These four phases of dress overlapped one another considerably; as there were also four major changes of headgear, the details of the steadily developing uniform are best considered in an orderly sequence.

Tunics

Irrespective of the tunic worn, the chasseur regiments were distinguished from one another by a facing of regimental colour, distributed to the regiments in the following manner.

Colour	Collar and cuffs	Cuffs only	Collar only
Scarlet	1	2	3
Yellow	4	5	6
Pink	7	8	9
Crimson	10	11	12
Orange	13	14	15
Sky Blue	16	17	18
Aurore	19	20	21
Capucine	22	23	24
Madder red	25	26	27
Amaranth	28	29	30
Chamois	31		

The dolman: despite the fact that this garment was never manufactured under the Empire, the dolman tunic was worn at least for full dress by all regiments prior to 1805. Probably a modified version of the 1791 *caracot*, it resembled the hussar dolman and had three rows of pewter buttons and between thirteen and eighteen rows of braid. The waist, back-seams, front vent, collar and cuffs were all liberally decorated with white lace. The version worn by the 5th Chasseurs had the added embellishment of shoulder-straps.

After 1804 we have the following information: inspection reports indicate the dolman was still commonly worn by the 3rd, 12th, 15th and 19th Chasseurs in 1804, the 1st, 6th, 7th, 9th, 10th, 20th and 24th Chasseurs in 1805 and the 4th, 5th and 16th Chasseurs in 1806. An existing garment in the Musée de l'Armée, Paris, attributed to the 4th Chasseurs, has the year 1808 stamped on the lining. Contemporary illustrations confirm the dolman to have been worn by the 1st Chasseurs during 1806 and the 5th Chasseurs as late as 1811.

3. Chasseur in full dress, 1802. Armed with the brand new *An IX*-pattern musketoon (the old 1786 model was also used for a good many years to come), this chasseur also boasts the 1801-pattern shako, so named despite having been in service since 1798. It was roughly the same shape as the one made regulation in 1806, but had the added features of a detachable peak and wrap-round turban. Though here the cords are plaited and looped about hooks at the sides, they would normally be wrapped around the wearer's body and knotted to keep it in place. The hair, although queued and plaited, was no longer powdered; this style of dressing persisted in the 15th and 26th Chasseurs as late as 1813. (Huen. Courtesy NAM)

The dolmans of NCOs and officers were identical to those of the men except that those of the officers would bear five rows of buttons and all lace would be silver. Rank distinctions are illustrated in detail in fig. 28; note that officers' lace could measure 14 mm or 23 mm in width, depending on rank. Finally, it should be mentioned that officers would supplement the dolman with an hussar-style *pélisse* if it took their fancy; contemporary illustrations record officers so attired of the 3rd, 5th and 27th Chasseurs as late as 1808, 1807 and 1810 respectively.

The habit-long: prior to 1806, the *habit-long* had been reserved for everyday and campaign wear but thereafter it was increasingly worn for full dress. This long-tailed and lapelled tunic was of identical colouring to the dolman save in the following particulars: the tails of the skirt were turned back to reveal the facing colour and ornamented, generally, with a green bugle-horn device. The collar and cuffs were devoid of the white lace which festooned the dolman, and would be piped in the opposite colour (i.e. green piping on a scarlet collar and scarlet piping on a green collar). The lapels, shoulder-straps and imitation pockets on the skirt would be piped in the facing colour.

While NCO's rank distinctions remained much the same, officer's rank was now indicated by epaulettes as illustrated in fig. 29. From surviving illustrations and records, it would appear that officers took to wearing the *habit-long* for full dress some time before the men did, and, though otherwise of identical cut, the officers' tunics frequently had the tips of the lapels rounded-off – no doubt a fashionable whim.

The Kinski: as of 1808, the single-breasted, short-tailed Kinski began to make its appearance. Fastening down to the waist by means of nine pewter buttons, and piped the length of the breast in the regimental colour, the tunic bore the same ornaments as the *habit-long* for all ranks. Simple, comfortable and devoid of the encumbering tails of that garment, it gradually replaced the *habit-long* for most functions until the advent of the 1812 *habit-veste*. Certain examples boast the addition of collar tabs of the opposing colour, serving to distinguish still more clearly the wearer's regiment. Officers

4. **Chasseur in campaign dress, 1800–2.** In service dress the chasseurs changed from the dolman or *caracot* to the more conventional *habit-long* in conjunction with a waistcoat and overalls. The waistcoat should officially have been single breasted, plain and white in summer and green in winter but staunch individualists that they were, the chasseurs adopted all manner of unofficial garments – in this case a plain red double-breasted type. (Similarly unofficial are his grey overalls which commonly replaced the tight Hungarian breeches, but which only became regulation in 1812.) (Benigni Courtesy NAM)

5. **Chasseurs of the élite company, 1805–6.** Created by decree of the *18 Vendémiaire An X* (1 October 1801) the first company of the first squadron was to be an élite unit, in imitation of the grenadiers of the infantry. As symbols of the élite status the men were accorded black bearskin colpacks in place of shakos; typically, each company so formed quickly took on the additional trappings of their infantry contemporaries, including red plumes, cords and tassels, fringed epaulettes and even the flaming grenade emblem (which was used to ornament the turnbacks, webbing, belt buckles and cartridge-pouches). lace on the breeches differed from the Hungarian knot to the bastion-shaped loop. (Benigni. Courtesy NAM)

ended to conserve their *habits-long* for walking-out dress though the Kinski would be worn for all other occasions.

The *habit-veste*: the 1812 *habit-veste*, introduced in 1813, was basically identical to the Kinski except that it had lapels. All ornaments and rank insignia remained precisely the same as those worn on the *habit-long*.

Beneath all the above-mentioned tunics, chasseurs wore sleeveless waistcoats, officially single-breasted and cut of white cloth for summer and green for winter, but, especially before 1812, endless different varieties were worn: double-breasted of white or scarlet cloth, single-breasted of red, green or regimental colour, and some were liberally festooned with lace and braid in imitation of the dolman. Buttons would either be identical to those of the tunic, pewter or silver, or covered in the same colour cloth as the waistcoat itself.

Troopers and NCO's were further issued with single-breasted, waist-length, green stable-jackets with collar and cuffs matching those of the *habit* and two flapless pockets at the waist. Examples of similar, double-breasted, versions also exist. Officers were issued a *surtout* for undress wear, closely ressembling the *habit* save that its skirt was devoid of turnbacks and its breast bare of lapels; fastening was generally be means of nine silver buttons.

Legwear

Throughout the Empire period, chasseurs most commonly wore green Hungarian breeches of hussar pattern; very close-fitting, they were decorated with piping 1 cm in width down the outer seams and with the same piping in the shape of either a Hungarian knot or a bastion loop about the twin vents on the front. They were further equipped with straps at the bottom of the leg to stop the breeches riding up inside the boots.

V. HUEN

7. Chasseur in stable-dress, 1805. The stable-jacket was dark green with collar and cuffs identical to those of the *habit-long*, it could be single or double-breasted with eight or nine pewter buttons per row. As of 1813, the garment became entirely dark green and single-breasted, fastening by means of ten pewter buttons. The trousers, of rough undyed cloth, opened laterally by means of cloth-covered or bone buttons down the outer seams; as the inclination towards trousers progressed, so versions appeared with button-up vents from the knee down only, to facilitate their wearing over boots. (Huen. Courtesy NAM)

On campaign the breeches were either replaced with coarse hide riding-breeches – *pantalons de cheval* – or covered by overalls. These overalls were of diverse cut and varied from undyed cloth through grey and green. They opened laterally and the outer seams bore eighteen pewter or bone buttons and regimental-coloured lace trim. The inner leg and cuffs of the trouser legs were reinforced with leather. Three-pointed flaps equipped with one or three buttons sealed hip pockets which were frequently attached to the front of the garment. Long after the overalls ceased to open laterally, they still frequently bore buttons, in much the same way as contemporary men's jackets carry redundant buttons at the cuff.

The 1812 regulations altered the stable-jacket solely in making it entirely dark green, while for the overalls they specified piping in lieu of lace down the outer seams.

6. Chasseurs of an élite and centre company, 1805. These chasseurs in undress uniform wear *surtout* tunics, overalls and fatigue-caps. The fatigue-caps, or *bonnets de police*, consisted of dark green turban and *flamme*; piped in the regimental colour, ornamented with a white bugle-horn patch and finished with a white tassel, the headdress was to last until 1813 when the pokalem version, as prescribed by the 1812 regulations, began to be issued. The scalloped cut of the leather inserts of the overalls is of particular interest. (Huen. Courtesy NAM)

10

Coats, capes and greatcoats

The chasseurs were first issued the tent-like green cavalry cape with hood. Thereafter followed the *manteau trois-quart* somewhat shorter, devoid of hood but with the addition of a short shoulder-cape stitched around the collar. In 1813 the *manteau-capote* was introduced; it was similar to the foregoing cape except for the addition of cuffed sleeves, and buttons down the front closure. The shoulder-cape was attached in such a way as to allow the wearer to wear the webbing outside the *manteau*, but underneath the cape. Officers wore similar capes save that in certain instances the shoulder-cape would be trimmed in silver lace. Officers also wore a full-length, double-breasted greatcoat—*redingote*—for foot duty; this was entirely green save for a collar of regimental colour.

Accessories

Chasseurs were generally shod in clogs for fatigues and riding-boots for all other duties. These boots were of Hungarian pattern, black leather and ornamented along the top with white lace and tassel. The 1812 regulations altered the decoration by specifying black leather trim and tassel. Spurs were originally of the detachable strapped variety, but they were later changed to the type that was screwed directly to the heel of the boot. Officers' service-dress boots were identical save for silver lace and tassel. For full dress, fancy goatskin boots, dyed red or green, were not uncommon. Officers' spurs were usually plated in silver or bronze.

For walking-out dress, shoes with large white metal buckles were worn with stockings. The stockings were white in summer and black or green in winter.

In full dress, cuffed gloves of white, or sometimes black for officers, were adopted in place of the wrist-length variety employed for most other duties.

9. Officer of a centre company, 1805–6. This fellow wears the 1801-pattern turbanned shako, with the addition of a chinstrap which made the cords unneccessary and purely decorative; the cartridge-pouch crossbelt has been covered in a red Morocco leather protective case, fastened by means of silver studs. The barrel-sash has been dispensed with and, in lieu of the very common *sabre à la hussarde*, he is armed with the officers'-pattern *sabre à la chasseur* – the difference being that the latter had additional pommel guards. (Wilke. Courtesy NAM)

Headgear

The main varieties of chasseur headgear are illustrated in fig. 30; for further details, readers are referred to the colour plates and their commentaries. The complex question of plumes and pompons requires discussion, however.

The pompon, or lentil-shaped disc as decreed by the 1812 regulations, referred to the wearer's squadron and company. There were endless variations, however, and following is the official guide: a red aigrette for the first company of the first squadron and a sky-blue, aurore or violet pompon for the first companies of the succeeding squadrons. The second company of the first squadron had a red pompon and the second companies of the remaining squadrons wore one of the same colour as the first but with a white centre, frequently bearing an

mbroidered squadron number. The first company f the first squadron would usually emphasize its lite status by wearing a red plume, their simple igrette being regarded as insufficiently different om the pompon of the second company.

The plumes referred to the wearer's regiment or rm. In the latter case it would simply be green, a olour universally indicative of light troops. In the ormer case, however, an anarchic situation existed whereby each regiment's plumes could be of either ne facing colour or green with tip or base of the acing colour. The proportion of the plume's length hat this facing colour occupied varied from a fifth o a third.

In undress uniform a *bonnet de police* of green was vorn by both troopers and officers. The cap itself of his headgear was laced in white and ornamented vith a white cloth patch of the bugle-horn device; he *flamme* or bag, left trailing or folded and tucked nto the cap, was piped in the regimental colour nd tipped by a white tassel. Officers' patterns were n the main identical, save that silver replaced vhite, but versions with a *flamme* of regimental olour are not unknown.

Webbing

This term includes the cartridge-case and crossbelt, musketoon-sling and crossbelt and the sabre's waistbelt and slings. Once again the reader is eferred to the line illustrations and captions for the precise specifications.

Chasseurs were at first issued with equipment of he 1801 pattern, which varied little from that ssued in 1786. The white buff leather (yellow for he 5th and 27th Chasseurs) crossbelts were 80 mm vide and both passed over the left shoulder, bound o one another by means of a spherical copper stud visible on the breast of many of the figures llustrated. All metal ornaments were copper apart rom the steel musketoon clip. The waistbelt and lings were manufactured from the same materials.

11. **Chasseur of a centre company in marching order, 1805–6. Again recorded during the German campaign of 1806: the shako has given way to the more comfortable** *bonnet de police* **whilst on the march; the leather inserts in his overalls are of 'wolf's teeth' cut, and the service chevron on his left upper arm designates between eight and ten years service. (Wilke. Courtesy NAM)**

Composed of three separate sections interlinked with copper rings, the waistbelt was adjustable by means of a buckle on the third section which permitted its length to be altered by folding the section back on itself. As of 1813, two amendments were made: the addition of a small copper hook to the first link-ring, from which the sabre would be hung by the first ring of its scabbard when the chasseur was on foot, and a bayonet frog immediately behind that ring.

Edged weapons

During the early Empire the *sabre à la hussarde* and *sabre à la chasseur* were simultaneously in use. The former varied considerably in the degree of curve to the edged blade, which was designed for both cut and thrust, and could have either an iron or a copper guard; its scabbard was of black leather with either iron or copper fittings. The latter

10. **Chasseur of an élite company in campaign dress, 1805–6. Recorded in Germany, this individual's uniform has several points of interest: the scarlet plume has been wrapped round n oilskin to preserve it from the elements, an alternative to packing it away in the portmanteau of the saddle, and the otherwise typical overalls have the added distinction of hip pockets with button-down flaps. He wears cuffed gloves, more normally reserved for full dress, and carries the 1786-pattern hussar musketoon. (Wilke. Courtesy NAM)**

ing in that iron was silver-plated and copper gilded. Further, embellishments were often embossed on the guard, scabbard fittings and blued steel blade. Their gold sword-knots came in two varieties, with either a flat lace or braid strap, and tassel composed either of slim filaments or chunky twisted coils.

Firearms

Originally, chasseurs carried the 1786-model hussar musketoon but this was slowly replaced by the updated *An IX* pattern, superseded in turn by the *An XIII* pattern. All were of varnished natural wood colour, had a steel barrel and were finished in copper throughout, save for the steel lock mechanism. Neither officers or trumpeters were armed with musketoons.

All ranks were supposedly issued with a brace of pistols apiece, but it is far likelier that only officers, trumpeters and, perhaps, NCO's were so armed. If troopers were issued pistols at all, they might well have a single weapon only, carried in the left saddle holster.

12. Trumpeter in No. 2 dress, 1806. Before the advent of the single-breasted, short-tailed Kinski tunic in 1808, an alternative to the *habit-long* was an otherwise identical but lapelless *surtout* tunic. Cut in the cloth of the regimental colour with facings of dark green, a popular means of more readily distinguishing musicians on the battlefield. The garment is embellished with white lace as would be facings of the *habit-long*. His shako is the 1806 model, augmented with chinscales and shako plate. Most usually this lozenge shape, many regiments' plates differed in having an embossed eagle upon them surmounting the regimental number which would be cut out of the metal. He is armed with 1786-model hussar sabre. (Huen. Courtesy NAM)

pattern had an N-shaped copper guard and a relatively shallow arc of curve; its scabbard was of black leather with copper fittings. As the years passed, the *An XI*-model light cavalry sabre gradually came to replace both preceding models. Its copper guard was composed of three bars and its scabbard was iron. Sword-knots were of white buff leather for all save the 5th and 27th Chasseurs who had yellow ones. The steel bayonet was 487 mm long; the 400 mm blade was triangular in shape and guttered on all three sides, to facilitate its removal from the victim's body.

Officers' sword patterns varied from the forego-

Saddles and Harness

The harnessing was of the Hungarian variety, the saddle covered in a white sheepskin schabraque edged in 'wolf's teeth' lace of the regimental colour. The portmanteau was green and its round ends were either laced or piped in white and ornamented with the regimental number in white. Bridles were also of Hungarian pattern. Trumpeters were supposed to have been issued black sheepskin schabraques to contrast with their grey mounts, but it is likely that as often as not they used the same type as the troopers.

The officers' harness comprised a Hungarian-pattern saddle, covered in leather and with cantle embellished in red or green Morocco leather, with red stirrup-leathers, and a green cloth schabraque piped in the regimental colour and laced in silver. This silver lacing varied in a similar manner to the rank chevrons: 27 mm for *sous-lieutenants* and *eutenants*, 40 mm for *capitaines* and one of 40 mm with one of 27 mm for all officers above that rank. The corner of the schabraque usually contained the regimental number embossed in silver, though officers of élite companies sometimes favoured a silver flaming grenade device. A more ornate leopard-skin schabraque was frequently employed by superior officers, though on campaign, they were replaced by simpler ones: plain green with a slim line of white piping about the edges or black bearskin decorated in the same manner as the troopers' sheepskin ones. Sometimes the schabraque was abandoned altogether, replaced by a black bearskin cover over the pistol holsters and a square green saddle cloth edged in silver lace beneath the saddle. All bridle strap buckles and ornaments were silver-plated.

War Records and Regimental Histories

The 1st Chasseurs à Cheval

Regimental history:

1651: Raised by Mis. d'Humières.

1733: Named the Conti Chasseurs.

1776: 25 March, became a regiment of dragoons.

1788: 17 March, renamed Régiment de Chasseurs d'Alsace.

1791: Became the 1er Régiment de Chasseurs.

1814: Renamed the Régiment de Chasseurs du Roi.

1815: Disbanded.

War record:

1805: Part of 1st Corps of the Grand Armée: Ulm, Amstetten, Mariazell and Austerlitz.

1806: Part of 3rd Corps of the Grand Armée: Auerstädt.

1808: Lowicz and Nasielsk.

1809: Part of the Armée d'Allemagne: Abensberg, Raab and Wagram.

1812: With the 1st Corps of the Grande Armée: Mohilev, Smolensk and Borodino.

1814: Took part in the defence of Maubeuge.

1815: Quatre-Bras and Rocquencourt.

The 2nd Chasseurs à Cheval

Regimental history:

1673: Raised 6 November by Le Chevalier de Fimarçon as a regiment of dragoons.

13. Colonel Baron Méda of the 1st Chasseurs, 1807. Resplendent in full dress uniform, this superior officer wears the 1806-pattern shako, richly ornamented with silver lace and equipped with a chinstrap of interlinking rings rather than the more familiar scaled versions; the *habit-long*, adopted by many officers long before the troopers, with twin fringed epaulettes as rank distinctions in place of the chevrons of the dolman, and lavishly ornate waistcoat and breeches. The boots are black although red or green pairs were not uncommon, and they bear matching lace to the shako. The heavily ornate belt buckle is embossed with bugle horn and laurel leaves; the sword-belt supports the 1803-model light cavalry sabre, normally reserved for chasseurs of the Imperial Guard. (Benigni. Courtesy NAM)

1788: Re-formed as chasseurs and named the Régiment de Chasseurs de Evêchés (No. 2).

1791: Renamed the 2eme Régiment de Chasseurs.

1814: Renamed the Régiment de Chasseurs de la Reine.

1815: Disbanded.

War record:

1805: With the Grande Armée: Dachau, Mariazell, Austerlitz, Auerstädt, Pultusk, Eylau, Mysziniec and Heilsberg.

1809: Part of the Armée d'Allemagne: Abensberg, Landshut, Eckmühl, Neumarkt, Ebensberg, Raab, Wagram and Znaïm.

1812–13: With the Grande Armée: Smolensk, Borodino, Mojaïsk, Wiasma, Bautzen, Wachau, Leipzig and Hanau.

14: Paris and Champaubert.

15: With the Armée du Rhin: action on the Suffel.

The 3rd Chasseurs à Cheval

Regimental history:

75: Founded by Charles du Fay at Philippsburg as a regiment of dragoons.

88: Became the Régiment de Chasseurs de Flandre (No. 3).

91: Renamed the 3eme Régiment de Chasseurs.

14: Renamed the Régiment de Chasseurs du Dauphin.

15: Disbanded.

War record:

05: With the Armée d'Italie: Caldiero.

07: Part of the Réserve de Cavalerie de la Grande Armée: Passenwerder and Heilsberg.

09: With the Armée d'Allemagne: Vilsbiburg, Essling and Wagram.

12–13: With the Grande Armée: Krasnoe, Borodino, Dresden and Leipzig.

14: Champaubert and Nangis.

15: With the Armée du Nord: Quatre-Bras and Waterloo.

The 4th Chasseurs à Cheval

Regimental history:

75: Raised 11 December by the Comte de Dreux-Nancré as a regiment of dragoons.

88: Became the Régiment de Chasseurs de Franche-Comté (No. 4).

91: Renamed the 4eme Régiment de Chasseurs.

14: Renamed the Régiment de Chasseurs de Monsieur.

15: Disbanded 16 July.

War record:

05: Part of the Armée de Naples: Padua, Venice and Saint-Michel.

06–12: Involved in pacifying Puglia and Calabria: Palmi.

12–13: With the Grande Armée: Niemen, Vitebsk, Krasnoe, Smolensk, Valoutina, Borodino, Berezina, Katzbach, Wachau, Leipzig and Glogau.

4. **Officers, 1807. The figure on the left is in morning dress with an officers'-pattern greatcoat, usually reserved for foot duty. Although here in felt bicorn, he might equally have worn the officers' version of the** *bonnet de police*, **identical to the men's save for silver lace and bugle-horn device. He carries the** *An XI* **pattern** *sabre à la chasseur*. **On the right is an individual in campaign dress, not necessarily of the élite company, since colpacks were popular throughout the officer class. The simple double-breasted waistcoat fastens to the left and has two flapless pockets. His pipe, embedded in its embroidered tobacco pouch, is looped about the gilded pommel of his** *An XI* **sabre. (Benigni. Courtesy NAM)**

15. **Chasseur in campaign dress, 1807. The** *habit-long* **had by now replaced the dolman almost entirely in most regiments, although the 5th and 27th Chasseurs clung to it until as late as 1811; prior to the advent of the Kinski tunic, it became the first distinctive item of dress of chasseur uniform as opposed to the hussar/chasseur style of the early Empire. This chasseur is armed with the** *An XI* **chasseur sabre, although many still carried the** *sabres à la hussarde* **and** *à la chasseur An IX*-**pattern. (Huen. Courtesy NAM)**

1814: Montmirail and Arcis-sur-Aube.

1815: With the Armée du Nord: Ligny and Waterloo.

The 5th Chasseurs à Cheval

Regimental history:

1675: Founded as a corps of dragoons.

1676: Became regular regiment of dragoons 13 March.

1788: Became Régiment de Chasseurs du Hainaut (No. 5).

1791: Renamed the 5eme Régiment de Chasseurs.

1814: Renamed the Régiment de Chasseurs d'Angoulême.

1815: Disbanded.

War record:

1805–7: With the Grande Armée: Munich, Wasserburg, Haag, Austerlitz, Schliez, Fürstenburg, Waren, Crewitz, Lübeck, Morhungen, Lobau, Krentzburg and Friedland.

16. Chasseur in campaign dress. 1809. He wears the single-breasted Kinski tunic introduced in 1808. Simple, short-skirted and comfortable, its use was widespread until the distribution of the 1812-pattern *habit-veste*. Ornaments remained the same as on the *habit-long*, shoulder straps for centre, and fringed epaulettes for élite, companies, as did the facing colour distribution. The twin chevrons of white lace indicate his rank to be that of *brigadier* (corporal). His shako has been covered in protective cloth, and his breeches with overalls strongly reminiscent of his fatigue-duty stable trousers. His firearm is the relatively new *An IX*-pattern musketoon. **(Benigni. Courtesy NAM)**

1808–13: Alcolea, Baylen, Burgos, Somosierra, Almaras, Medellin, Torrigos, Talavera, Cadiz, Bornos, Alhambra, El-Coral, Caracuel, Olmedo, Hillesca, Burgos and Vitoria.
1813: With the Grande Armée: Jüterbock, Dennewitz, Mockern, La Partha, Leipzig and Hanau.
1814: With the Armée d'Espagne: Orthez and Toulouse. Campaign of France: Remagen, La Chaussée, Châlons, Mormant, Troyes, Bar-sur-Aube, Arcis-sur-Aube, Sommepius and Saint-Dizier.

The 6th Chasseurs à Cheval

Regimental history:
1676: Created 4 October by the Etats du Languedoc as a regiment of dragoons and named the Languedoc-Dragons.
1788: Became Régiment de Chasseurs du Languedoc (No. 6).

1791: Renamed the 6eme Régiment de Chasseurs.
1814: Renamed the Régiment de Chasseurs de Berry
1815: Disbanded 30 November.

War record:
1803–4: Part of the Armée d'Italie.
1805–8: With the Armée de Naples: Castel-France Occupation of Calabria and the Abruzzo.
1809–11: Part of the Armée d'Italie: Sacile, La Piav San-Michel and Wagram.
1812: With the 3rd Corps of Cavalry of the Grand Armée: Smolensk, Borodino and Malojaroslawetz.
1813: Part of the 1st Corps of Cavalry of the Grand Armée: Bautzen, Wachau and Leipzig.
1814: Remained with the 1st Corps: Champaubert ar Vauchamps.
1815: With the Armée du Nord: Mont-Saint-Jea Waterloo and Rocquencourt.

The 7th Chasseurs à Cheval

Regimental history:
1745: Created 15 August as a mixed corps of foot ar horse light troops and named the Volontaires Royau
1747: Renamed the Légion Royale.
1776: 25 March, regiment disbanded and troo dispersed into existing infantry and dragoon reg ments.
1779: 29 January, four squadrons of the old Légio Royale reformed as the 1er Régiment de Chasseurs Cheval.
1784: 8 August, transformed again into a mixed cor and renamed the Régiment de Chasseurs des Alp (No. 1).
1788: 17 March, infantry became chasseurs à pied ar cavalry renamed the Régiment de Chasseurs Picardie (No. 7).
1791: Became the 7eme Régiment de Chasseurs.
1814: Renamed the Régiment de Chasseurs d'Orléan
1815: Disbanded.

War record:
1805–7: Part of the 7th Corps of the Grande Armé Embs, Jena, Wismar, Hameln, Eylau, Königsber and Heilsberg.
1809: With the Armée d'Allemagne: Pfaffenhoffe Raab and Wagram.
1810–11: Fuentes d'Onoro.

17. Chasseur of an élite company, 1813. Newly accoutred fo the most part in accordance with the 1812 regulations, th individual wears the lapelled *habit-veste*, otherwise identical the Kinski; the grenadier-pattern 1812 shako, with red upp band and side chevrons, and the non-regulation pompon an plume of scarlet. He carries the *An XI* sabre, and his 1812-pa tern belt has the recently introduced bayonet frog and a sma hook to which the first ring of the steel scabbard would attached so as to facilitate the sabre's wear when the chasseu was on foot. **(Huen. Courtesy NAM)**

1812–13: With the Grande Armée: Polotsk, Drissa, Berezina, Danzig, Bantzen, Liegnitz, Katzbach, Reichenbach and Leipzig.

1814: Bar-sur-Aube.

1815: With the Armée du Rhin: action on the Suffel.

The 8th Chasseurs à Cheval

Regimental history:

1749: A mixed corps formed of the Arquebusiers de Grassin, Fusiliers de la Morlière and Volontaires Bretons.

1757: Divided into the Volontaires de Flandre and the Volontaires du Hainaut.

1762: Became the Légion de Flandre.

1776: 25 March, disbanded in same manner as the Légion Royale.

1779: Re-formed from four squadrons of the old Légion de Flandre as the 2eme Régiment de Chasseurs à Cheval.

18. **Officer in full dress, 1813.** At this period, officers' dress was not very different from the men's except of finer quality and with silver ornaments. The dark-green trousers, embellished with twin strips of regimental-coloured lace, have replaced the Hungarian breeches and the webbing is black leather edged in silver instead of plain white. (Huen. Courtesy NAM)

19. **Officer in campaign dress, 1813.** The 1812 regulation make no mention of the bearskin colpack, but it is wide recorded that officers retained theirs for the duration of th wars. Beneath the Morocco-leather cover, this officer crossbelt is probably prescribed by those same decrees: dark-green leather with silver lace edging. The *redingote* coa worn in place of cape, lacked the folded down collar regimental colour that was typical of previous models bu otherwise was the same. Some authorities maintain tha though normally dark green, the cuffs were sometimes also regimental colour or piped therein. (Benigni. Courtesy NAM

1784: Became a mixed corps again and renamed th Régiment de Chasseurs des Pyrénées (No. 2).

1788: Infantry companies severed and cavalry rename the Régiment de Chasseurs de Guyenne (No. 8).

1791: Renamed the 8eme Régiment de Chasseurs.

1814: Renamed the Régiment de Chasseurs de Bourbo

1815: Disbanded at Perpignan 3 December.

War record:

1805: Part of the 2nd Corps of the Grande Armée: Uln Gratz and Nordlingen.

1806–11: Part of the Armée d'Italie: Sacile, Montebell La Piave, Saint-Michel, Raab and Wagram.

1810–11: Stationed in the Tyrol.

1812: With the Grande Armée: Dnieper, Ostrown Krasnoe, Smolensk, Borodino, Mojaïsk and Wir kowo.

1813: Remained with the Grande Armée: Möcker Bautzen, Dresden, Goldberg and Leipzig.

1814: Saint-Dizier, Champaubert, Berry-au-Bac, L Fère-Champenoise and Paris.

1815: The Sambre passage, Ligny, Villers-Cotterets an Versailles.

The 9th Chasseurs à Cheval

Regimental history:

1757: Created 1 April as a mixed corps by division o preceding regiment and named the Volontaires d Hainaut.

1762: Renamed the Légion de Hainaut.

1768: Renamed the Légion de Lorraine.

1776: Disbanded 25 March.

1779: Reformed as the 3eme Régiment de Chasseurs Cheval.

1784: Became mixed corps and renamed the Régimen de Chasseurs des Vosges (No. 3).

1788: Renamed the Régiment de Chasseurs de Lorrain after infantry companies were axed.

1791: Renamed the 9eme Régiment de Chasseurs.

1814: Renamed the Régiment du Colonel-Général.

1815: Disbanded, 21 September.

War record:

1801: With the Armée de Naples: Saint-Euphémie Monteleone.

1808: Reggio, Messina and Scilla.

P. Benigni

1809: With the Armée d'Italie: Brenta, Piave, Saint-Michel, Leoben, Raab and Wagram.

1810: Part of the Armée de Naples during the Calabrian campaign.

1812–13: With the Grande Armée: Borodino, Wiasma, Lützen, Bautzen, Dresden, Löwenberg, Goldberg, Leipzig and Hanau.

1814: Champaubert, Château-Thierry, Brienne, Montmirail, Sézanne, Reims, La Ferté, Montereau, Melun and Paris.

1815: Ligny and Waterloo.

The 10th Chasseurs à Cheval

Regimental history:

1758: Mixed corps created, 7 May, for the Comte de Clermont and named the Volontaires de Clermont-Prince.

1763: Renamed the Légion de Clermont-Prince.

1766: Renamed the Légion de Condé.

1776: Disbanded, 25 March

1779: Reformed of four squadrons of the Légion de Condé as the 4eme Régiment de Chasseurs à Cheval.

1784: Reformed as a mixed corps and named the Régiment de Chasseurs des Cévennes (No. 4).

1788: Became the Régiment de Chasseurs de Bretagne (No. 10) after infantry companies had been axed.

1791: Renamed the 10eme Régiment de Chasseurs.

1815: Disbanded 30 August.

War record:

1805–7: Part of the 6th Corps of the Grande Armée: Elchingen Jena, Hoff, Eylau, Deppen and Friedland.

1808–13: With the Armée d'Espagne: Medina-del-Rio-Seco, Medellin, Albacon, Talavera, Almonacid, Ocaña, Malaga, Baza and Vitoria.

1813: With the Grande Armée: Leipzig.

1814: With the Armée des Pyrénées: Orthez, Viella and Toulouse.

1814: Part of the 6th Corps of the Grande Armée: Montereau and Fontvannes.

The 11th Chasseurs à Cheval

Regimental history:

1762: Created 11 January as a mixed corps named the Volontaires Etrangers de Würmser.

1762: Renamed 21 December as the Volontaires de Soubise.

1766: Renamed the Légion de Soubise.

1776: Disbanded 25 March.

1779: Re-formed of four squadrons of the old Légion de Soubise as the 5eme Régiment de Chasseurs à Cheval.

1781: Became a mixed corps again and renamed the Régiment de Chasseurs du Géraudan (No. 5).

1788: Renamed the Régiment de Chasseurs de Normandie (No. 11) after the infantry companies wer separated from the regiment.

1791: Renamed the 11eme Régiment de Chasseurs.

1815: Disbanded.

War record:

1805: Part of the 4th Corps of the Grande Armée: Uln and Austerlitz.

1806–7: With the Grande Armée: Jena, Lübeck, Eylau Danzig, Guttstadt, Heilsberg and Friedland.

1809: With the Armée d'Allemagne: Eckmühl, Ratis bonne and Znaïm.

1810–12: Part of the Armées d'Espagne et du Portugal Fuentes d'Onoro.

1812: With the 2eme Corps de Réserve de Cavalerie o the Grand Armée: Borodino and Winkowo.

1813: With the Grande Armée: Lützen, Bautzen Leipzig and Hanau.

1814: Vauchamps.

1815: Part of the 3rd Corps of the Armée du Nord Waterloo.

The 12th Chasseurs à Cheval

Regimental history:

1769: Mixed corps created after the conquest of Corsica and named the Légion Corse.

1775: Renamed the Légion du Dauphiné. Disbanded 25 March.

1779: Re-formed of four squadrons of the old Légion Corse as the 6eme Régiment de Chasseurs à Cheval.

1784: Became a mixed corps once again and named the Régiment de Chasseurs des Ardennes (No. 6).

1788: Renamed the Régiment de Chasseurs de Champagne (No. 12) after infantry companies had been separated from the regiment.

1791: Renamed the 12eme Régiment de Chasseurs.

1815: Disbanded.

20. Chasseur of an élite company in campaign dress, 1813. Sketched during the 1813 campaign, this illustration after a contemporary artist is of interest on several counts. Though the overalls are as prescribed in the 1812 regulations, dark green, reinforced with black leather and opening laterally by means of pewter buttons, the vent ornamented with piping of the regimental colour, his accoutrements are far from regular. Firstly, a scarlet *aigrette* should have replaced the pompon and plume of the élite companies on the 1810 shako, and all the obsolete cords and tassels were strictly abolished; secondly, in place of the 1812-pattern waistbelt, he wears a pattern reminiscent of that of heavy cavalry and lancers, and in a most unorthodox way; over his tunic. Lastly, in place of the sheepskin schabraque issued to troopers, his saddle has the added feature of a dark-green saddle-cloth, edged in white, an item normally reserved for officers' horse furniture. **(Benigni. Courtesy NAM)**

War record:

1805–7: With the 3rd Corps of the Grande Armée: Auerstädt, Czentoschau, Golymin, Okunin, Czarnowo, Biezun, Heilsberg and Gross-Krug.

1808: With the Armée du Rhin: occupation of Silesia, Westphalia, Saxony and Franconia.

1809: With Montbrun's Division of the Armée d'Allemagne: Eckmühl, Ratisbonne and Wagram.

1812: Part of the Grande Armée: Wilia Pass, Rudnia, Krasnoe, Borodino and Winkowo.

1813: Könnern, Katzbach and Leipzig.

1814: Part of Saint-Germain's Division during campaign of France: Bar-sur-Aube.

1815: With the Armée du Nord: Ligny and Waterloo.

The 13th Chasseurs à Cheval

Regimental history:

1792: Created from squadrons of the Légion des Americains et du Midi and named 13eme Régiment de Chasseurs.

1794: 13eme (bis) Régiment de Chasseurs created from two squadrons of the Légion du Nord and the Volontaires.

1795: 13eme and 13eme (bis) Chasseurs amalgamated as 13eme Régiment de Chasseurs, 11 April.

1815: Disbanded at Niort and Belfort.

War record:

1805–7: With the Grande Armée: Ulm, Braunau, Halberstadt, Passewalk, Nasielk and Eylau.

1809: Part of the Armée d'Allemagne: Essling, Engereau, Wagram, Hollabrunn and Znaïm.

1810–13: Fuentes d'Onoro, Mondego, Los Arapilos, Villodrigo and Tordesillas.

1813: Four squadrons with the Grande Armée: Dennewitz.

1814: 4th, 5th and 6th squadrons took part in the campaign of France: Bar-sur-Aube and Montereau. 1st, 2nd and 3rd squadrons with the Armée des Pyrénées: Orthez and Toulouse.

1815: 1st, 2nd and 3rd squadrons: Belfort. Remainder with the Corps d'Observation du Jura.

The 14th Chasseurs à Cheval

Regimental history:

1793: Created from four squadrons of the Hussards des Alpes, one company of the Hussards de l'Egalité and a company of the Hussards de la Mort. Named the 14eme Régiment de Chasseurs.

1815: Disbanded.

War record:

1805: With the Armée d'Italie: Caldiero and Vicence.

1806: Part of the Armée de Naples: Gaëta.

1807: Part of the 8th Corps of the Grande Armée: Stralsund.

1809: With the Armée d'Allemagne: Ratisbonne, Eckmühl, Ebersberg, Essling and Wagram.

1812–13: Part of the Armée de Portugal: Nava-del-Rey, Los Arapilos, Monasterio, Villodrigo and Vitoria.

1813: With the Grande Armée: Dresden, Leipzig and Hanau.

1813–14: Siege of Belfort.

1814: Saint-Dizier, Brienne, Bar-sur-Seine, Champaubert and Montmirail.

The 15th Chasseurs à Cheval

Regimental history:

1793: Created from the Chasseurs de Beysser and several irregular companies of the Western départements. Named the 15eme Régiment de Chasseurs.

1815: Disbanded.

War record:

1805–6: Part of the Armée d'Italie: Caldiero and Tagliamento.

1807: With Colbert's Division of the Grande Armée: Lomitten.

1808–9: Part of the Armée d'Espagne: passage of the Guadarrama, of the Esla, Banos Pass and Alba-de-Tormes.

1810–11: With the Armée de Portugal: Torres Vedras.

1811–12: Some squadrons with the Armée d'Espagne: Sanguessa and Villodrigo. Remainder with the Armée du Nord and the Corps d'Observation de réserve.

1813–14: Pampeluna, Vitoria, Orthez and Toulouse. Remainder with the Grande Armée: Leipzig, Lützen, Weissenfels and Arcis-sur-Aube.

The 16th Chasseurs à Cheval

Regimental history:

1793: Created 7 March from the Chasseurs Normands de Labretèche and named the 16eme Régiment de Chasseurs.

1814: Disbanded 12 May.

1815: Re-formed 16 April from Belgian volunteers. Dissolved 1 July.

War record:

1805: With the Grande Armée: Amstetten, Posalitz, Vischau and Austerlitz.

1806–7: Part of the Grande Armée: Jena, Lübeck, Hoff, Eylau and Königsberg.

1809: With the Armée d'Allemagne: Landshut, Ebersberg, Essling, Raab and Wagram.

1812: With the Grande Armée: Vilna, Mohilew, Ostrowno, Vitepsk, Smolensk, Borodino and Krasnoe.

1 Trooper, 5th Chasseurs, campaign dress, 1806
2 Trumpeter, 1st Chasseurs, full dress, 1802
3 Colonel, 5th Chasseurs, full dress, 1804

ANGUS McBRIDE

A

1 Brigadier, 1st Chasseurs, campaign dress, 1804–05
2 Chef de Musique, 7th Chasseurs, full dress, 1805–06
3 Subaltern, 1st Chasseurs, service dress, 1806

B

1 **Sous-Officier, 10th Chasseurs, full dress, 1809**
2 **Trumpeter, 6th Chasseurs, service full dress, 1809**
3 **Subaltern, 16th Chasseurs, full dress, 1809**

C

1 Trooper, 13th Chasseurs, campaign dress, 1806
2 Trumpeter, 7th Chasseurs, service dress, 1810–12
3 Officer, 4th Chasseurs, campaign dress, 1809

D

ANGUS McBRID

1 Trooper, 26th Chasseurs, full dress, 1809–12
2 Trumpeter, 24th Chasseurs, campaign dress, 1809
3 Superior Officer, 20th Chasseurs, full dress, 1812

E

1 Trooper, 7th Chasseurs, campaign dress, 1811
2 Trumpeter, 11th Chasseurs, full dress, 1810
3 Superior Officer, 14th Chasseurs,
   summer walking-out dress, 1810–12

F

1 Trooper, 6th Chasseurs, service dress, 1813–14
2 Trumpeter, 12th Chasseurs, campaign dress, 1812
3 Subaltern, 8th Chasseurs, regulation full dress, 1813–14

1 Trooper, 2nd Chasseurs, campaign dress, 1813–14
2 Trumpeter, 27th Chasseurs, full dress, 1813–14
3 Subaltern, 19th Chasseurs, campaign dress, 1813–14

13: Part of the Grande Armée: Lützen, Kulm and Leipzig.

14: La Rothière, Champaubert, Vauchamps, La Fère-Champenoise and Paris.

The 17th Chasseurs à Cheval

Regimental history:

793: Created from the Chevau-Légers de West-Flandre and named the 17eme Régiment de Chasseurs.

794: Disbanded.

315: Re-formed at Bordeaux on 16 August from the 15eme Régiment de Chasseurs and named the Régiment de Chasseurs d'Angoulême.

The 18th Chasseurs à Cheval

Regimental history:

793: Created 9 May from the 1er Régiment de Chevau-Légers Belges and the Compagnie de Dragons de Bruxelles. Named the 18eme Régiment de Chasseurs.

794: Disbanded 18 July.

315: Re-formed as the Régiment de Chasseurs de la Sarthe (No. 18).

The 19th Chasseurs à Cheval

Regimental history:

793: Created from the Chasseurs de la Légion de Rosenthal and several irregular companies on 10 June. Named the 19eme Régiment de Chasseurs.

314: Disbanded.

War record:

304–6: With the Armée d'Italie: Caldiero, San-Pietro, Treviso and Tagliamento.

306–7: With the Grande Armée: Marienwerder, Danzig and Stralsund.

309: Part of the Armée d'Allemagne: Neumarkt, Ebersberg, Essling and Wagram.

310–11: Part of the Armée d'Illyrie.

312: With the Grande Armée: Ostrowno, Smolensk, Borodino.

313: Malojaroslawetz, Wiasma, Krasnoe. Danzig, Torgau, Weissenfels, Bautzen, Dresden, Gorlitz, Borach and Leipzig.

313–14: With the Armée d'Italie: Caldiero, Mincio and Taro.

The 20th Chasseurs à Cheval

Regimental history:

793: Created from the Légion du Centre (or de Luckner) and named the 20eme Régiment de Chasseurs.

814: Disbanded.

War record:

1806–7: Part of the 7th Corps of the Grande Armée: Jena, Eylau, Guttstadt and Heilsberg.

1809: With the 2nd Corps of the Armée d'Allemagne: Pfaffenhausen, Amstetten, Raab and Wagram.

1810–12: With the Armées d'Espagne et du Portugal: Fuentes d'Onoro and Altafulla.

1812–14: Part of the 2nd Corps of the Grande Armée: Polotsk, Borisow, Berezina, Katzbach, Leipzig, Hanau, Montmirail and Montereau.

The 21st Chasseurs à Cheval

Regimental history:

1793: Formed as the 21eme Régiment de Chasseurs from a corps of irregular hussars.

1814: Disbanded.

War record:

1805: Part of Lasalle's Brigade of the 5th Corps of the Grande Armée: Wertingen, Ulm and Austerlitz.

1806: With Treilhard's, then Lasalle's Brigade of the Grande Armée: Saalfeld, Jena, Spandau, Prentzlow and Pultusk.

1807: With the 5th Corps of the Grande Armée: Ostrolenka and Ostrowno.

1809–14: With the Armée d'Espagne: Arzobispo, Ocana, the Andalusian expedition, siege of Badajoz, Gebora, Albufera, Los Arapilos, Vitoria, Orthez and Toulouse.

Detailed records of the histories of regiments numbered 22 to 26 inclusive are not given in the official French Ministry of War lists. Formed following the Directory re-organisations of 1791–92, these units, although formed as chasseurs, were assigned to *Guides* duties with the staffs of various army corps commanders.

The Plates

A1 Trooper of the 5th Chasseurs in campaign dress, 1806
Although chasseurs of this period are most commonly represented wearing an hussar-style dolman tunic, it was in fact the practice to resort to the *habit-long* as shown here for undress and campaign wear, the dolman being reserved for more formal occasions. Of interest is his curious headgear, the 1801-pattern shako (so named despite having been

P. Benigni

26

. Chasseurs, 1814. In stark contrast to our first illustrations f chasseurs' ostentatious early dress is this representation of he uniforms of conscripts despatched to fight the 1814 ampaign of France. Dressed in the manner in which they left he depot, the figure on the left has only the 1812 version of atigue-cap, the Pokalem, as headgear and a stable jacket, (at his period entirely dark green) as tunic; his companion has ared somewhat better, having received an 1810 model shako nd 1812 pattern *habit-veste*. Both waistbelts lack bayonet frogs nd bayonets. Such was the state of dress and equipment of the rench army at this period that it can be firmly stated that hese two are fortunate indeed to own what little they have. Benigni. Courtesy NAM)

fficially recognised as early as 1798), with its distinctive detachable peak and wrap-round tur-an, strongly reminiscent of the hussars' *mirliton* ap. This regiment clung to several features of dress nore readily associated with the hussars until well nto the Empire: this pattern of shako until 1807, he dolman tunic as late as 1811 and, here in 1806, he 1786-pattern hussar sabre and musketoon. 'urther, the 5th Chasseurs, in common with the 7th, had the distinction of yellow webbing in place f the usual white. (Illustration after Benigni)

2 *Trumpeter of the 1st Chasseurs in full dress, 1802*
Despite the fact that the dolman tunic was never nanufactured during the course of the Empire, the hasseurs painstakingly conserved them for full-ress wear regardless of the fact that they dated ack to 1791. Recorded in 1802, this uniform is nown to have been worn throughout the 1805 ampaign even though an inspection report dated 2 July 1805 assures us that all the dolmans of this egiment were worn-out and that none remained in he depot. This tunic becomes even more interest-ng when one notices that it bears five rows of uttons, in place of the normal three reserved for all anks below officer class, and, although the familiar ractice has been followed of making the tunic of he same colour cloth as the facings of the men, it as a scarlet collar instead of the more normal dark reen one, an anomaly perpetuated until 1809 lespite the advent of the Kinski tunic. He wears a artridge-pouch and crossbelt, even though trum-eters were never equipped with musketoons, and lso, a sabretache, an uncommon accessory for hasseurs. (Illustration after Cmndt. Bucquoy)

3 *Colonel of the 5th Chasseurs in full dress, 1804*
The 5th Chasseurs is credited with being the first egiment to adopt the colpack fur cap, which was to

prove enormously popular with officers, irrespec-tive of company, and later as headdress for all troopers of the élite companies (in imitation of the tall bearskins sported by grenadiers in the in-fantry). The loose hanging bag, in this instance cut in the regimental colour, was also occasionally made of plain white cashmere. As the use of chinscales increased, the less practical cap lines or cords were retained solely for the sake of ornamen-tation.

22. Chasseur of the 1st Regiment, 1815. With the First Restoration of the Monarchy under Louis XVIII in 1814, the 1st Chasseurs were renamed the *Chasseurs du Roi* and equipped with crested helmets as an élitist gesture to the first light cavalry regiment of the realm. This illustration depicts a trooper so equipped at the beginning of the ill-fated Hundred Days campaign of 1815. Having removed the epaulettes and aiguillettes with which they were also issued in the Emperor's absence, the chasseurs bent their will to the *CHASSEURS DU ROI* inscription on the helmet plate and, by means of a little judicious filing, erased the R and O and achieved *CHASSEURS DU I*, a neat compromise. (Benigni. Courtesy NAM)

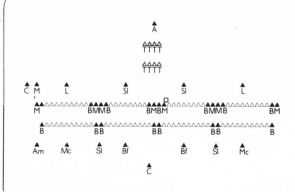

23. Squadron of chasseurs in battle order. This formation provided a squadron with its maximum frontage and minimal two-man depth. A regiment of four squadrons extended in this manner might be arranged in line or echelon, in which event the squadron numbers would read from one to four, right to left, or in column, in which case the squadrons would be in first, third, fourth and second order, reading from front to back.

Officers' dolman tunics were essentially the same as the troopers' save for five rows of buttons, supporting eighteen rows of braid, and, albeit infrequently, a silver lace *cadre* surrounding the whole. Interestingly, although both the 5th and 27th Chasseurs indulged in shoulder straps on their troopers' tunics, their officers did not follow suit, but adopted the more normal method of chevron rank distinctions on the sleeve with matching bastion-shaped lace on the breeches. In this case, we see that a colonel's rank was designated by alternating lace strips of 23 and 14 mm in width. He carries the officers'-pattern hussar sabre, dating well back to the Republic, rather than the more elaborate *sabre à l'allemande* with which many of his brother officers would be armed. Officers of the 5th are well documented as having worn a *pélisse* as late as 1807, which was more naturally associated with their hussar-style dress, but which was a rare

accessory under the Empire. Officers' full-dress boots were frequently made of red or green goatskin, though here they are a conservative black. (Illustration after Benigni)

B1 Brigadier of the 1st Chasseurs in campaign dress 1804–5

As mentioned above, the dolman was not manufactured during the Empire and those recorded must have been either the chasseurs' 1791-pattern *caracot*, with thirteen rows of braid, or hussar pattern dolmans, boasting no less than eighteen loops of braid. On the NCO's dolman, which was identical to the troopers', rank was indicated by twin chevrons of white lace for *brigadiers* (corporals), single silver chevrons for *maréchaux-des-logis* (sergeants) and twin silver chevrons for *maréchaux des-logis-chefs* (sergeant-majors). On campaign, the tight Hungarian breeches of the trumpeter in *A*

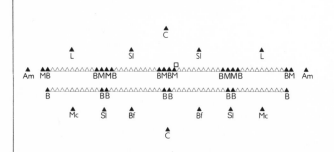

24. Lead squadron of chasseurs in *colonne serré* **order.** Drawn up for this column formation, the squadrons advanced on a fully extended front, one behind the other at a distance of sixteen metres, lead horse to lead horse. The depth of a two-rank line was six metres.

Master key to figs. 23, 24, 25, 26, 27

B: *Brigadier* (**corporal**)

Bf: *Brigadier-fourrier* (**quarter-master corporal**)

M: *Maréchal-des-logis* (**sergeant**)

Mc: *Maréchal-des-logis-chef* (**sergeant-major**)

Am: *Adjutant-major* (**regimental sergeant major**)

Sl: *Sous-lieutenant* (**second lieutenant**)

L: *Lieutenant* (**first lieutenant**)

C: *Capitaine* (**captain**)

A: *Adjutant* (**adjutant**)

T: *Trompette* (**trumpeter**)

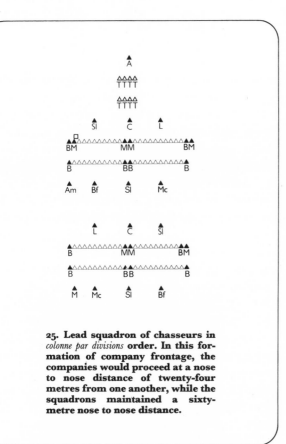

25. **Lead squadron of chasseurs in** *colonne par divisions* **order. In this formation of company frontage, the companies would proceed at a nose to nose distance of twenty-four metres from one another, while the squadrons maintained a sixty-metre nose to nose distance.**

26. **Lead squadron of chasseurs in** *colonne par peletons* **order. Of troop frontage, the individual troops and companies of a squadron would keep even distance of twelve metres, lead horse to lead horse, for this formation. Squadrons, measured in the same manner, would precede one another by fifty-nine metres.**

27. **Lead squadron of chasseurs in column by fours. In this close formation, troops and companies of a squadron would keep equal distance of twelve metres nose to nose from one another, while following squadrons maintained a gross, ie. lead horse to lead horse, distance of a hundred metres.**

were replaced by hide riding breeches or covered by overalls. These last were of many varieties, but generally dark green or grey, reinforced with leather and laced the length of the outer seams in the regimental colour; they fastened laterally by means of eighteen bone, pewter or cloth-covered buttons. Clearly visible here is the strap which, passing beneath the foot, would attach to a calf button in order to stop the breeches riding up. The oilskin round both shako and plume is to preserve

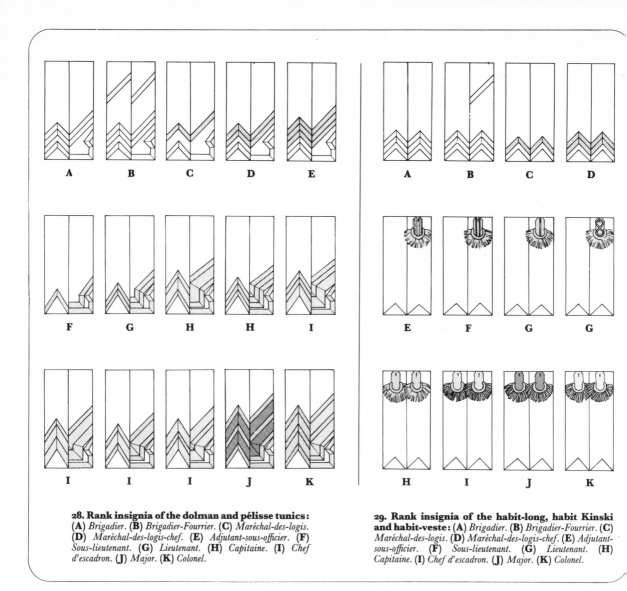

28. Rank insignia of the dolman and pélisse tunics:
(**A**) *Brigadier.* (**B**) *Brigadier-Fourrier.* (**C**) *Maréchal-des-logis.*
(**D**) *Maréchal-des-logis-chef.* (**E**) *Adjutant-sous-officier.* (**F**)
Sous-lieutenant. (**G**) *Lieutenant.* (**H**) *Capitaine.* (**I**) *Chef
d'escadron.* (**J**) *Major.* (**K**) *Colonel.*

**29. Rank insignia of the habit-long, habit Kinski
and habit-veste:** (**A**) *Brigadier.* (**B**) *Brigadier-Fourrier.* (**C**)
Maréchal-des-logis. (**D**) *Maréchal-des-logis-chef.* (**E**) *Adjutant-
sous-officier.* (**F**) *Sous-lieutenant.* (**G**) *Lieutenant.* (**H**)
Capitaine. (**I**) *Chef d'escadron.* (**J**) *Major.* (**K**) *Colonel.*

them from the elements. The musketoon, not yet replaced by the *An IX* pattern, is slung from the crossbelt so that it could be both fired and loaded without having to be unclipped. The hair queue, which was disappearing fast at the onset of the nineteenth century, remained popular with the more traditional regiments and was still fashionable as late as 1811 in the 20th, and 1813 in the 15th and 26th Chasseurs. (Illustration after Rousselot/Duboys de l'Estang)

B2 Chef de Musique of the 7th Chasseurs in full dress, 1805–6

The principal priority for musicians was, in theory, that they be readily distinguishable from the mass of troops, for which reason they were issued uniforms of identical cut but of contrasting colour to the men's, and rode greys (as did some officers). The basic rule was therefore to reverse the colours, the musicians wearing the facing colour where the troops wore dark green and vice versa – but nowhere was individuality, extravagance, dandyism and out-and-out foppery more tolerated than in the élitist light cavalry. What chance had the humble shako when colpacks or czapskas became available? The briefest glance at chasseur musicians leaves the observer with the impression that their uniforms must have been redesigned very frequently. Tunics, headgear, and ornamentation offer a bewildering spectacle to which no rhyme or eason can be attached. This figure is a perfect example; assuming that his old pink dolman with green facings has worn out, it seems likely that, pink cloth being a trifle scarce in the midst of a campaign, his coat was run up from the most easily obtainable, indigo-blue cloth. Yet a Negro *timbalier* has been recorded by Boeswilwald in the same year with full Eastern regalia in the correct colours; furthermore, if pink cloth was scarce, where did the trefoils and colpacks appear from? Musicians at this time wore uniforms like this one, but with white lace in lieu of silver, trumpeters almost the same but with lace only about the collar (those of the élite company added scarlet fringed epaulettes) and yet less than a year later we have evidence of pink tunics and even pink shakos.

The argument for expediency clearly only goes so far, but it is rather the self-indulgence of the regimental colonels, vying with one another for the most dashing heads of column that brought about the Emperor's decree in 1810 to the effect that henceforth a dark green Imperial Livery should be universal. (Illustration after Cmndt. Bucquoy/Carl/Boeswilwald)

B3 Subaltern of the 1st Chasseurs in service dress, 1806
Although German documents record that many of the 1st Chasseurs wore dolmans during the campaigns of 1805 and 1806, the garment was fast disappearing in favour of this *habit-long*, hitherto reserved for No. 2 dress. The officers' pattern was basically the same as the men's save for silver ornaments and buttons, and sometimes, as in this instance, the fashionable rounding-off of the tops of the lapels. Rank was now indicated by epaulettes, all ranks below *chef d'escadron* wore only one, on the left shoulder. At this period the felt shako originally issued under the Consulate became regulation and was termed 'the 1806 pattern'; it was devoid of turban, had a fixed peak, stood 160 mm tall and measured 230 mm in diameter at the top. Far too simple for contemporary tastes, it was often discarded for the colpack or was elaborately embroidered in silver. As the years passed, it became taller, embellished with black velvet and ornamented with a plate of white metal. Pompons of silver, surmounted by plumes of black or dark green tipped in the regimental colour, were promptly added – along with chinscales which the

original design omitted. In place of breeches, officers took to wearing trousers: at first steel grey and laced and buttoned down the outer seams, they soon lost their buttons but retained the lace in the form of twin strips down the outer leg. Gradually, the steel grey gave way to dark green as ground fabric, and so they remained throughout the Empire. But this is not to say that breeches were ever totally replaced; they remained in service for grand occasions. Sabres *à la hussarde* and *à l'allemande* had by this time given way to the officers' pattern *An XI* sabre *à la chasseur* with its gilded copper fittings. (Reconstruction)

C1 Sous-officier of the 10th Chasseurs in full dress, 1809
The rather old-fashioned and cumbersome *habit-long* began to decline in popularity with the introduction of the eminently practical Kinski tunic in 1808. Single-breasted and short-tailed, it was perhaps the most sensible garment yet devised for increasingly mobile warfare, and it was the forerunner of the 1812 *habit-veste* which was to transform the dress of the French Line army into a more appropriate one for the new century. However, old traditions die hard and the ornate, sleeveless waistcoat worn beneath the tunics remained a firm favourite: in theory single-breasted, plain-fronted, white in summer, dark green in winter, it was frequently personalised by being cut in the regimental colour, scarlet or dark green, and either emblazoned with braid and lace or, at the very least, cut double-breasted. Notice also, that all the ornamentation of the *habit-long* has been transferred to the new garment: the single silver chevron on his left upper-arm denotes between eight and ten years service; the cuff chevrons indicate his rank and the scarlet fringed epaulettes proclaim his élite company status. Further evidence of his belonging to the first company of the first squadron is his bearskin colpack and scarlet pompon and plume. These élite companies were created following the decree of 18 October 1801 (*18 Vendemiaire An X*) which accorded their members the bearskin cap as testimony of their distinction. Not to be outdone by the infantry grenadiers, the chasseurs promptly followed this with epaulettes, plumes, cords and colpack bags of scarlet; perhaps sensing they were on to a good thing, many companies even appended the flaming

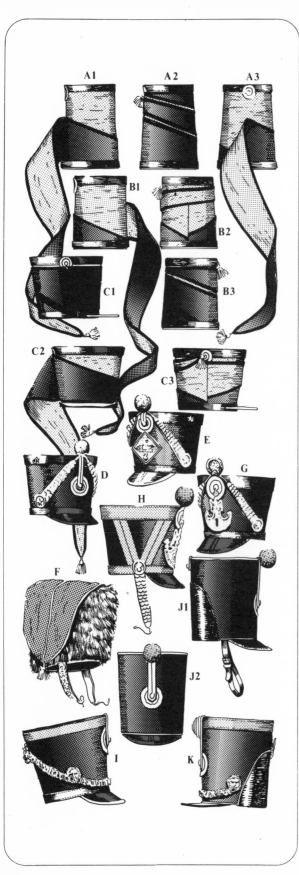

30. Chasseur headgear, 1790–1815. (A) The *mirliton* cap *c.* 179[0] with *flamme* unravelled and viewed from the front (1); wit[h] *flamme* wrapped round to reveal the black protective side a[nd] worn in service dress, again from the front (2) and finall[y] again unravelled, but viewed from the right hand side (3[)]. Height: 240 mm. (B) the *mirliton* cap *c.* 1795 with *flamme* unravelle[d] viewed from the front (1); with *flamme* wound anticlockwise t[o] reveal the facing colour, viewed from the left hand side (2) an[d] lastly, with *flamme* wound clockwise, again viewed from left (3[)]. Height: 220 mm. (C) The 1801-model shako with *flamme* woun[d] clockwise (1); with *flamme* unravelled, viewed from front (2[)] finally, with *flamme* wound anti-clockwise (3). Height: 190 mm[;] width: 220 mm. (D) The 1806 model shako, 1805–07. Heigh[t] 160 mm; width 230 mm. (E) The 1806-model shako, 1807–12. (F[)] The bearskin colpack, 1805–14. (G) The 1810-model shak[o.] Height: 220 mm; width: 270 mm. (H) The 1812-pattern éli[te] company shako. Height: 190 mm; width: 245 mm. (I) Officers[’] pattern 1810-model shako. (J) Troopers'-pattern 1812 cylindr[i-] cal shako (1) and (2). (K) Officers'-pattern 1812 cylindrica[l] shako.

grenade device to their turnbacks, cartridge[?] pouches and crossbelts. Perhaps the most extrem[e] example was the company of chasseurs sketched b[y] Suhr in Hamburg in 1812 who had gone so far as t[o] attach a party of bearded sappers to their ranks[,] armed with lances flying scarlet pennants! (Illus[-] tration after Benigni)

*C2 Trumpeter of the 6th Chasseurs in service full dress[,]
1809*

In keeping with the beggar-my-neighbour policy o[f] presenting increasingly exotic heads of column, th[e] dress of this trumpeter leaves only the green plum[e] to indicate to which branch of the army he belong[s.] Fantasy has clearly been allowed full rein in th[e] choice of ground colour for the tunic in order t[o] compete more flaboyantly with the no doub[t] equally pompous splendour of their neighbourin[g] regiment. Although one must allow for th[e] difficulty in purchasing bolts of cloth of the mor[e] obscure facing colours, such as aurore, amaranth o[r] capucine, by the regiments in the field, it is hard t[o] reconcile this with the fact that scarlet was at thi[s] period one of the most expensive colours available[.] (Illustration after Rousselot/Marckolsheim MS)

C3 Subaltern of the 16th Chasseurs in full dress, 1809[.]
This full-dress figure illustrates a rather typica[l] chasseur officer of the period: despite the in[-] troduction of the comfortable and simple Kinsk[i] tunic, most officers were loathe to part with thei[r] smarter *habit-long* which became reserved for ful[l] and walking-out dress. Although it might seem[?]

outdated when worn with braided waistcoat and Hungarian breeches, it should be borne in mind that though the garments remained the same, the cut changed considerably over the years, becoming 'snappier' and closer-fitting with the evolution of civilian fashions. Notice the webbing: there would seem to have been a great latitude in the choice of accoutrements, and webbing of black, green or red Morocco leather was quite acceptable. At first only edged in silver lace with silver studs along the body, the crossbelt and cartridge-pouch became increasingly ornate; silver devices of Imperial N's, eagles, shields embossed with the regimental number, and lions' heads began to abound to such an extent that the owners were obliged to protect their costly investment with red or crimson leather covers (see *B3*) when on campaign. He carries the officers' pattern *An XI* sabre, finished in silver rather than gilded. (Illustration after Rousselot)

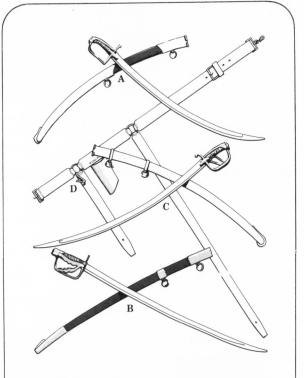

31. **Troopers' edged weapons and accessories. (A) The 1786-model hussar sabre. Blade: 800 mm. (B) The 1801-model chasseur sabre. Blade: 900 mm. (C) The *An XI* light cavalry sabre. Blade: 845 mm. (D) The 1812-pattern waistbelt and bayonet frog. Overall length: 107 cm. width: 40 mm; width of slings: 35 mm; length of first sling: 340 mm; length of second: 970 mm.**

D1 Trooper of the 13th Chasseurs in campaign dress, 1806

This trooper affords us a rearview of the *habit-long*. The rather sack-like early patterns were getting slimmer and the turnbacks of the skirt, which were originally literally pinned back and tended to appear baggy, were becoming increasingly narrow and were stitched along their entire length. Although originally functional, the pockets in the tails of the skirt were now obsolete, and piping in the distinctive *soubise* shape merely mimicked their presence. The buckle at the rear of his 1806-pattern shako allowed the headdress to be tailored to individual size. (Illustration after Rousselot)

D2 Trumpeter of the 7th Chasseurs in service dress, 1810–12

Of particular interest are the button loops on the collar and cuffs of his reversed-colour Kinski tunic. Authorities conflict on this detail: although Würtz and the Börsch Collection record similar loops about alternating breast buttons for the years 1808 and 1809, Vanson and Jolly both confirm their disappearance in 1810 and accord the tunic white lace about collar and cuffs only. The white chevrons on his left upper arm denote between sixteen and twenty years service. Finally, according to both Jolly and Vanson, a similar 1806-pattern shako, covered in pink cloth, bedecked with white cords and tassels and surmounted by a white plume, would be utilised in full dress. (Illustration after the Marckolsheim MS).

D3 Officer of the 4th Chasseurs in campaign dress, 1809

In contrast to the subaltern in *C3*, this fellow illustrates the much simplified dress that officers would adopt when on active service. The bearskin colpack, now stripped of all ornament, reveals the manner in which the chinscales would be hung on a small hook at back of the headgear when not in use. A plain double-breasted waistcoat replaced the elaborately braided full-dress version, and steel grey trousers the Hungarian breeches. Trousers, increasingly in vogue, were rapidly becoming acceptable as full-dress items, in which event they would be identical to those shown here, but cut in dark green. (Illustration after Rousselot)

33

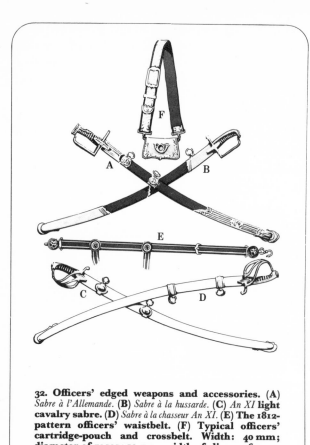

32. Officers' edged weapons and accessories. (A) *Sabre à l'Allemande.* **(B)** *Sabre à la hussarde.* **(C)** *An XI* **light cavalry sabre. (D)** *Sabre à la chasseur An XI.* **(E) The 1812-pattern officers' waistbelt. (F) Typical officers' cartridge-pouch and crossbelt. Width: 40 mm; diameter of roses: 50 mm; width of slings: 26 mm; length of buckles: 48 mm; width of piping: 6 mm.**

E1 Trooper of the 26th Chasseurs in full dress, 1809–12

From its inception, the 1806-pattern shako was disliked by the chasseurs and each regiment stretched the rules by having theirs constructed somewhat differently: with or without slim leather chevrons on the sides, with added chinscales, with the innovation of a folding neck-cover stitched to the interior headband, but all shakos had a tendency to be taller and broader than those prescribed by regulation. The most common shako plate was lozenge-shaped, embossed with an Imperial eagle and with the regimental number cut out of its white metal. However, rising-sun plates, such as the one illustrated have been recorded on shakos of the 25th, 26th and 27th Chasseurs; their origin was no doubt the same as the czapskas acquired for the bandsmen (see the trumpeter in *G2*). This individuality spread to the plumes and pompons and it is therefore nearly impossible to decode the meaning of the colour-combination. All that can be specified with any certainty is that the pompons related to the companies and the plumes to the regiments. The preponderance of red-based regimental colours makes for difficulty in distinguishing one from the other: aurore from orange or capucine from scarlet or garance from crimson.

This regiment has opted for the Hungarian knot instead of the inverted bastion shape to ornament the breeches.* (Illustration after Rousselot, Martinet)

E2 Trumpeter of the 24th Chasseurs in campaign dress, 1809

With his reversed-colour Kinski, this trumpeter has the unusual distinction of wearing sky blue overalls in place of the more habitual dark green or grey patterns; though these lack the familiar leather insert on the inside leg, this individual has painstakingly appended leather cuffs to the trouser legs to save them from wear and tear. A further feature is that he still carries the old *sabre à la chasseur* instead of the new *An XI* model worn by the trooper in *E1*; the manufacture and distribution of new equipment was so haphazard and slow that enemy arms, looted from captured arsenals and supply trains, were frequently pressed into service.* (Illustration after Suhr)

E3 Superior officer of the 20th Chasseurs in full dress, 1812

The officers, like the troopers, took readily to the Kinski tunic and, between 1808 and the advent of the 1812 *habit-veste*, it was the most widespread tunic in use. All ornaments and decoration were identical to those of the *habit-long* with the sole exception of the use of collar patches of regimental colour in place of piping (although this was not universal practice, it was certainly frequent and a more effective means of discerning the wearer's regiment). His white plume designates his rank as do the epaulettes, for only officers above the rank of *chef d'escadron* were permitted the *contre-épaulette* and white, instead of dark green or black, plume. In passing, note the cross and ribbon of the *Légion*

*Readers are referred to the note at the close of the section on regimental histories. Since these units served as *Guides*, a possible explanation of non-regulation uniform features may lie in the known tendency of senior commanders to indulge in a certain freedom of imagination when uniforming their *entourages*.

l'Honneur pinned to his breast. (Illustration after Rousselot)

51 Trooper of the 7th Chasseurs, in campaign dress, 1811
Recorded in Spain, this uniform was probably the most frequently seen of the chasseurs' wardrobe during a campaign. Of primary interest are the protective cloths applied to the shako and musketoon lock, an extremely common practice to prevent damage from the elements but, in the case of the shako, quite possibly to conceal its foreign origin. Evidence in support of this possibility is his black leather crossbelt which is clearly not of French manufacture. No doubt assigned to foot duty, perhaps for lack of horses, he has discarded his sabre. The *An XI*-pattern light cavalry sabre's waistbelt had the innovation of a small hook attached to it precisely to facilitate its wear when on foot. His collar, though devoid of collar patch, bears buttons conceivably intended for fastening to the collar of the greatcoat. (Illustration after Feist/El Guil)

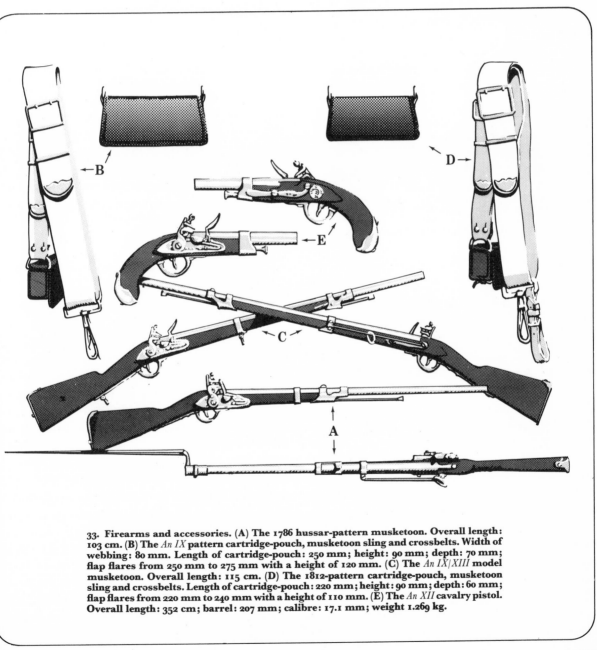

33. Firearms and accessories. (A) The 1786 hussar-pattern musketoon. Overall length: 103 cm. (B) The *An IX* pattern cartridge-pouch, musketoon sling and crossbelts. Width of webbing: 80 mm. Length of cartridge-pouch: 250 mm; height: 90 mm; depth: 70 mm; flap flares from 250 mm to 275 mm with a height of 120 mm. (C) The *An IX/XIII* model musketoon. Overall length: 115 cm. (D) The 1812-pattern cartridge-pouch, musketoon sling and crossbelts. Length of cartridge-pouch: 220 mm; height: 90 mm; depth: 60 mm; flap flares from 220 mm to 240 mm with a height of 110 mm. (E) The *An XII* cavalry pistol. Overall length: 352 cm; barrel: 207 mm; calibre: 17.1 mm; weight: 1.269 kg.

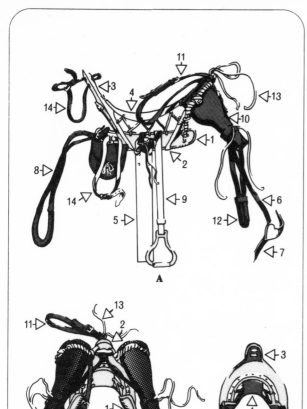

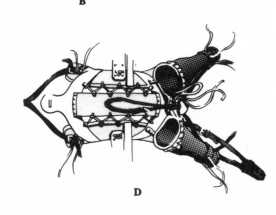

34. **The tree and accessories of the Hungarian saddle. (A) Side view. (B) Full on. (C) Rear view. (D) Top view. 1 Side panels. 2 Pommel. 3 Cantle. 4 Seat. 5 Girth. 6 Breastplate. 7 False-martingale. 8 Crupper. 9 Stirrup leathers. 10 Pistol holsters. 11 Musketoon strap. 12 Musketoon boot. 13 Cape thongs. 14 Portemanteau thongs.**

F2 Trumpeter of the 11th Chasseurs in full dress, 1810

Rare at this late date, he wears the *habit-long* in place of the more comfortable Kinski tunic. That this was the case for the troopers of this regiment as well and not simply a full-dress fancy of the musicians is borne out by a report dated 20 September 1809, which describes the *habits-long* of a detachment arriving from France. Seemingly further placing this figure at an earlier date than that specified is the fact that he carries the 1786 pattern *sabre à la hussarde* instead of the more expected *sabre à la chasseur* or *An XI* pattern. Further, though long obsolete, cords and tassels still ornamented the shako for full dress occasions. (Illustration after Marckolsheim Ms)

F3 Superior officer of the 14th Chasseurs in summer walking-out dress, 1810–12

As can be seen, off-duty wear differed little from that normally worn save for the replacement of the colpack or shako by a felt bicorn. It should be added, however, that at this late date this was probably the sole use to which the *habit-long* was put, it being that much smarter than the Kinski tunic most popularly adopted by officers. (Illustration after Rousselot)

G1 Trooper of the 6th Chasseurs in service dress, 1813–14

In 1810 a new pattern of shako was decreed, taller and broader than ever: 220 by 270 mm. It is considered likely, however, that the chasseurs used the one prescribed for the infantry, a more stable 190 mm tall and 240 mm in diameter. In direct accordance therefore with that issued to grenadiers, chasseurs of élite companies were equipped with models having red in lieu of black leather bands and chevrons. This is not to say that colpacks were abolished, indeed most élite companies retained them throughout the Empire, but the new levies were so equipped. This trooper wears the *habit-veste*, as prescribed by the 1812 regulations, basically the same as the Kinski, but fastening down the breast by means of hooks and eyes; the lapels could be buttoned back, as shown here, or buttoned across to left or right. The red chevron on the left upper arm designates eight to ten years' service. These same regulations ordered the attachment of a bayonet frog to the waistbelt. Of greatest interest are this

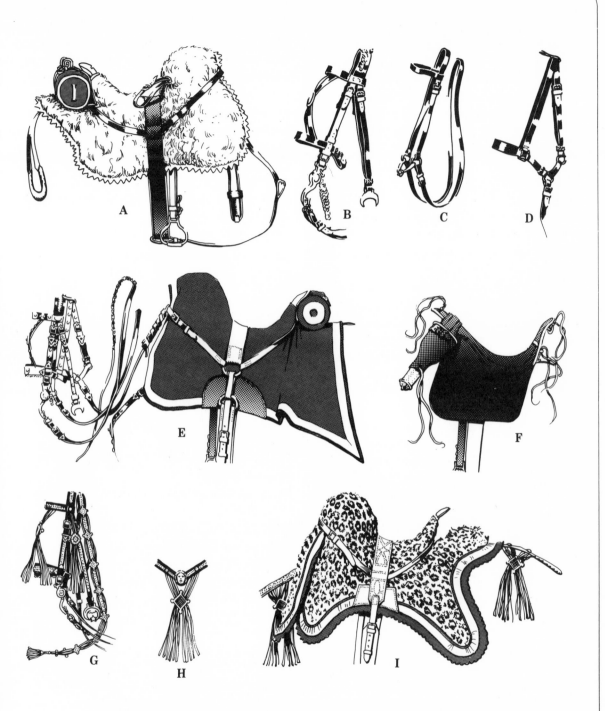

35. Saddles, harness and bridles. (A) Trooper's pattern Hungarian saddle and schabraque. (B) Troopers' Hungarian bridle. (C) Troopers' Snaffle bridle. (D) Parade halter of troopers' bridle. (E) Complete horse furniture of officers' mounts. (F) Officers' pattern Hungarian saddle in leather. (G) Bridle of superior officers' parade dress horse furniture. (H) Breastplate to G. (I) Superior officers' Hungarian saddle with leopard skin schabraque.

trooper's overalls: firstly, in place of the strip of regimental coloured lace, we see a band of white lace; secondly, the leather insert on the inside leg is gone, while the cuffs of the legs have been raised and ornamented with white piping describing the contour of the full-dress Hungarian boot. All in all, the garment has come a long way from the laterally opening overalls we first saw, and now fairly successfully mimics breeches and boots. (Illustration after Benigni)

G2 Trumpeter of the 12th Chasseurs in campaign dress, 1812

The Marckolsheim MS records trumpeters of this regiment in the year 1810 in the reversed-colour habit of musicians, but 1812 found them again dressed in the sky-blue tunic and breeches they had sported in 1804. This is perhaps explained by the fact that the 10th and and 11th Chasseurs also wore crimson tunics, and the need to distinguish between them, especially between the 12th and 10th, prompted the change. A further embellishment was the acquisition of czapskas for the musicians, seen here wrapped in oilskin against the elements; uncovered, it was crimson with a broad white strip of lace about the top edge. Most unusual was its copper plate which, in place of the familiar rising-sun pattern, described not an Imperial but a Polish eagle, so large that its wings spread across the width of the side panels. (Illustration after Rousselot)

G3 Subaltern of the 8th Chasseurs in regulation full dress, 1813–14

Though the officers clung jealously to their bearskin colpacks, the 1812 regulations prescribed a shako of identical pattern to that of the troopers. Subalterns were no longer to wear plumes, but rather pompons of company colour and, though cords and tassels would not be tolerated, the upper band of the shako could be ornamented with silver lace or embroidery. Despite this gracious generosity of the war department towards the vanity of their junior officers, most of them perversely opted for a conservative band of black velvet. All rank insignia and detail of the Kinski tunic were transferred to the new *habit-veste*. While the Hungarian breeches remained the only officially recognised form of legwear, dark-green trousers laced in the re-gimental colour were far more popular. Note that

the predilection of officers for personalised webbing has here reached its apogee, being entirely worked in silver with not a trace of leather remaining visible. (Illustration after Hilpert)

H1 Trooper of the 2nd Chasseurs in campaign dress 1813–14

At the beginning of the Empire, chasseurs wore the dark-green cavalry cape with attached hood or the so-called three-quarter length cape, of considerably narrower cut than its predecessor, with a short shoulder-cape stitched about the collar but devoid of the hood. The 1812 regulations, applicable as of 1813, specified a new garment, more in the line of a greatcoat, called the *manteau-capote*. Unlike the previous version, this one had the luxury of cuffed sleeves and a button-up front. The shoulder cape described on the three-quarter length cape was carried over to this design, enabling the wearer to strap his webbing over the coat rather than beneath it, as had to be done with the hooded cape. Note the updated overalls; like those worn by the trooper in G1 they are devoid of leather insert but have cuffs of fawn leather on the legs. Both of the individuals should officially have been wearing overalls similar to those of the trooper in D1, but with piping in place of lace in accordance with the 1812 regulations. (Reconstruction)

H2 Trumpeter of the 27th Chasseurs in full dress, 1813–14

With a view to regularising the dress of musicians, an Imperial Livery was devised and ordered as of 1811. The Imperial lace was to be manufactured in two versions, the one for horizontal and the other for vertical use, and to be composed of alternating Imperial N's and eagles. These came in several varieties – green devices on yellow ground, vice-versa or alternating – but always separated by black thread and bordered in red. Such a costly garment smacking of a sovereign's royal livery did not please the individualist regimental colonels, who therefore tended to have tunics of correct cut manufactured, but in the same colours as the previous Kinski. The 27th Chasseurs, ex-*Chevau-légers d' Arenberg* and relative latecomers to the ranks of French chasseurs, were apparently never issued with the 1810-model shako and this fellow therefore wears the old 1806 pattern with the addition of chinscales; though old, it none the less affords him the luxury of decorative cords and tassels and the now abolished pompon and plume. (Illustration after Benigni)

H3 Subaltern of the 19th Chasseurs in campaign dress, 1813–14

Clinging tenaciously to his bearskin colpack in the face of the austere regulation shako, this officer wears the new *habit-veste* identical to that of the rank and file save for the ornaments. Notice also his overalls of similar pattern to those of the trooper in *G1*, with cuffs giving the semblance of boots, except that the lace is silver in place of white. (Illustration after Rousselot)

SOURCES

Anon., *Manoeuvres de la Cavalerie*

H. Bouchot, *L'Epopée du costume militaire française*

Cmndt. Bucquoy (Ed.), *Les uniformes du 1er Empire*

French Ministry of War, *Historique des corps de troupe de l'armée française*

Dr Hourtouille (Ed.), *Soldats et uniformes du 1er Empire*

Job, *Tenue des troupes de France*

Marx, *Tableaux synoptiques des manoeuvres de la Cavalerie*

J. Regnault, *Les aigles perdus*

Col. H. C. B. Rogers, *Napoleon's Army*

L. Rousselot, *L'Armée française*

Various issues of *La Giberne*, *Le Passepoil* and *Gazette des uniformes*

Légendes

1 Chef d'escadron en grande tenue, 1800, d'aprés Hoffmann. **2** Officiers, 1800. Ils portent le schako enfin autorisé en 1806 aprés plusiers années d'utilization non-officiel, et le caracot de 1791. **3** Chasseur en grand tenue, 1802, avec le schako modèle 1801. **4** Chasseurs vers 1800–1802, en tenue de campagne comprenant l'habit-long et les surculottes. **5** Chasseurs d'une compagnie d'élite, 1805–1806. Les compagnies d'élite, créés par décret du 18 octobre 1801, étaient formées par la première compagnie du premier escadron de chaque régiment de la cavalerie. **6** Chasseurs d'une compagnie d'élite et du centre, 1805, en petite tenue: surtouts, pantalons de cheval et bonnets de police. **7** Chasseur en tenue d'écurie, 1805. En général, les chasseurs préféraient les sabots pour cette tenue. **8** Officier d'une compagnie d'élite, 1805–1806: prévue d'origine pour les compagnies d'élite seulement, le colback fut vite adopté par la plupart des officiers de chaque régiment. **9** Officier d'une compagnie du centre dans le schako à flamme modèle 1801, 1805–1806. **10** Chasseur d'une compagnie d'élite en tenue de campagne, 1805–1806. Nous remarquons que son plumet est enveloppé de toile ciré. **11** Chasseur d'une compagnie du centre en tenue de route, 1805–1806. **12** Trompette en petite tenue, 1806. **13** Le Colonel-Baron Méda du 1er Chasseurs en grande tenue, 1807. **14** Officier en petite tenue du matin, redingote et chapeau bicorne (à gauche) et officier subalterne en tenue de campagne (à droite), 1807. **15** Chasseur en tenue de campagne, 1807 le dolman est toujours porté. **16** Brigadier en tenue de campagne, 1809. Il porte l'habit Kinski qui a apparu vers 1808. **17** Chasseur d'une compagnie d'élite, 1813, habillé dans l'ensemble d'aprés les régulations de 1812, y compris le shako à bandes rouges. **18** Officier en grande tenue, 1813. A part l'effet des détails, nous pouvons constater que l'uniforme des officiers et de la troupe ne ressemble beaucoup. **19** Officier en tenue de campagne, 1813. Bien que le tarif général pour 1813 ne le mentionne pas, il semble que cette coiffure fut retenue par la majorité des officiers; il porte la redingote à la place du manteau-capote. **20** Chasseur d'une compagnie d'élite en tenue de campagne, 1813, d'aprés un portrait contemporain. Il démontre plusieurs détails de costume qui sont en opposition avec le Réglement de 1812.

21 Chasseurs de 1814 en tenues courantes des conscrits maléquipés. **22** Chasseur du 19ème Régiment, 1815; au début des Cent-jours, ils portaient toujours le casque que Louis XVIII leur a présenté lors de la Première Restauration. **23** Escadron de chasseurs en ordre de bataille: B=Brigadier; Bf=Brigadier-Fourrier; M=Maréchal-des-logis; Mc=Maréchal-des-logis-chef; Am=Adjutant-Major; Sl=Sous-Lieutenant; L=Lieutenant; C=Capitaine; A=Adjutant; T=Trompette. **24** Premier escadron de chasseurs en colonne serré: légende du personnel pareil à **23** ci-dessus. **25** Premier escadron de chasseurs en colonne par divisions: légende du personnel pareil à **23** ci-dessus. **26** Premier escadrons de chasseurs en colonne par pelotons: légende du personnel pareil à **23** ci-dessus. **27** Premier escadron de chasseurs en colonne par quatres: légende du personnel pareil à **23** ci-dessus. **28** Galons de grades pour le dolman et la pélisse: A=Brigadier; B=Brigadier-Fourrier; C=Maréchal-des-logis; D=Maréchal-des-logis-chef; E=Adjutant-sous-officier; F=Sous-Lieutenant; G=Lieutenant; H=Capitaine; I=Chef d'escadron; J=Major; K=Colonel. **29** Galons de grades pour l'habit-long, l'habit Kinski et l'habit-veste: légende pareil à **28** ci-dessus. **30** Coiffures de chasseurs, 1790–1815; A=Bonnet de hussard ou Mirliton vers 1790: (1) à flamme trainante de grande tenue, (2) à flamme enroulée de petite tenue et (3) à flamme trainante vue di droite; B=Mirliton vers 1795: (1) à flamme trainante vue de face, (2) à flamme enroulée de manière à demontrer la couleur particulière au régiment, vue de gauche, et

(3) à flamme enroulée de petite tenue, vue de gauche; C=Schako modele 1801: (1) à flamme enroulée de grande tenue, (2) à flamme trainante, vue de face, et (3) à flamme enroulée de petite tenue; D=Schako porté entre 1805 et 1807 de modèle 1806; E=Schako porté entre 1807 et 1812 de modèle 1806; F=Le colback en peau d'ours, 1805–1814; G=Le schako modèle 1810; H=Le schako modèle 1812 des compagnies d'élite; I=Le schako d'officiers-modèle 1810; J=Le schako cylindrique de la troupe, 1812; K=Le schako cylindrique d'officiers, 1812.

31 Armes blanches et bufflèteries de la troupe: A=Sabre à la hussarde, 1786. B=Sabre à la chasseur, 1801. C=Sabre de cavalerie-légère, modèle An XI. D=Ceinturon à porte-baïonnette, modèle 1812. **32** Armes blanches et bufflèteries d'officiers: A=Sabre à l'Allemande. B=Sabre à la hussarde. C=Sabre de cavalerie-légère, modèle An XI. D=Sabre à la chasseur, modèle An XI. E=Ceinturon modèle 1812. F=Giberne et porte-giberne typique. **33** Armes à feu et accessoires: A=Mousqueton de hussard, modèle 1786. B=Giberne, porte-giberne et banderole porte-mousqueton, modèle An IX. C=Mousqueton de cavalerie-légère, modèle Ans IX/XIII. D=Giberne, porte-giberne et banderole porte-mousqueton, modèle 1812. E=Pistolets An XIII. **34** Arçon et accessoires d'une selle à la Hongroise: A=Profil droit. B=Vue de Face. C=Vue d'arrière. D=Vue par-dessus. 1=Bande d'arçon. 2=Arcade de pommeau. 3=Arcade de trousseqin à palette. 4=Siège. 5=Sous-ventrière ou sangle. 6=Poitrail avec coeur. 7=Fausse-martingale de poitrail. 8=Croupière. 9=Etrivières avec étrier à la hussarde. 10=Fonte. 11=Courroie porte-mousqueton. 12=Botte pour le canon du mousqueton. 13=Lanières de fixation du manteau. 14=Lanières de fixation du porte-manteau de trousseqin. **35** Harnachements des chevaux: A=Selle à la Hongroise et schabraque de la troupe. B, C et D=Bride à la Hongroise, bridon et licol de parade de la troupe. E=Harnachement complet de cheval d'officiers. F=Selle d'officiers à la hussarde en cuir. G, H et I=Bride garnie de plaques tressées et de lanières, poitrail et schabraque en peau de panthère d'officiers supérieurs.

Notes sur les planches en couleurs

A1 Chasseur du 5eme Régiment en tenue de campagne, 1806. Il porte l'habit-long et le schako modèle 1801. **A2** Trompette de 1er Chasseurs en grande tenue, 1802. Le dolman fut gardé jusqu'en 1807. **A3** Colonel du 5ème Chasseurs en grande tenue, 1804. Ce régiment était le premier à porter le colback comme coiffure.

B1 Brigadier du 1er Chasseurs en tenue de campagne, 1804–1805. **B2** Chef de Musique du 7ème Chasseurs en grande tenue, 1805–1806. **B3** Officier subalterne du 1er Chasseurs en tenue de service, 1806, vêtu de l'habit-long.

C1 Sous-officier du 10eme Chasseurs en grande tenue, 1809, qui porte l'habit Kinski. **C2** Trompette du 6ème Chasseurs en grande tenue de service, 1809. Il est vêtu de la manière flamboyante des têtes de colonne. **C3** Officier subalterne du 16eme Chasseurs en grande tenue, 1809; il porte l'habit-long, et une giberne et porte-giberne se son propre goût.

D1 Chasseur en du 13ème Régiment en tenue de campagne, 1806, qui nous montre l'arrière-vue de l'habit-long. **D2** Trompette du 7ème Chasseurs en tenue de service, 1810–1812. Remarquez les ganses qui ornent son habit Kinski de couleurs inversées. **D3** Officier du 4ème Chasseurs en tenue de campagne, 1809. Ceci est en exemple de l'uniforme porté quotidiennement par les officiers en tenue de service.

E1 Chasseur du 26eme Régiment en grande tenue, 1809–1812; dés sa consécration officielle le schako modèle 1806 ne plaisait déjà plus, et chaque régiment confectionait un modèle particulier. **E2** Trompette du 24eme Régiment en tenue de campagne, 1809. Il porte des surculottes bleu-ciel ce qui est insolite pour l'époque. **E3** Officier supérieur du 20eme Chasseurs en grande tenue, 1812; remarquez les pattes de couleur sur son col.

F1 Chasseur du 7eme Régiment en tenue de campagne, 1811; cet uniforme fut noté en Espagne. **F2** Trompette du 11eme Chasseurs en grande tenue, 1810. Curieusement, il semble que tout cet régiment a continué à porter l'habit-long jusqu'en septembre 1809. **F3** Officier supérieur du 14eme Chasseurs en tenue de société, 1810–1812.

G1 Chasseur du 6eme Régiment en tenue de service, 1813–1814, qui porte le schako modèle 1810. **G2** Trompette du 12eme Chasseurs en tenue de campagne, 1812. Il est coiffé de la coiffure à la polonaise dite czapska. **G3** Officier subalterne du 8eme Chasseurs en grande tenue réglementaire, 1813–1814; il porte l'habit-veste et le schako modèle 1812.

H1 Chasseur du 2eme Régiment en tenue de campagne, 1813–1814; il porte le manteau-capote de 1812. **H2** Trompette du 27eme Chasseurs en grande tenue, 1813–1814; il porte la Livrée Impériale décrét par l'Empereur en 1810. **H3** Officier subalterne du 19eme Chasseurs en tenue de campagne, 1813–1814. Il porte l'habit-veste de 1812 et une coiffure non-réglementaire, le colback.

Überschrift

1 Chef d'escadron in grosser Uniform 1800 nach Hoffmann. **2** Offiziere, 1800, tragen schon den Schako, der nur 1806, nach vielen Jahren im gebrauch bei der Truppe, vorschiftsmässig aufgenommen wurde, und die M1791 caracot. **3** Chasseur in grosser Uniform 1802 mit dem sogenannten 'M1801 Schako'. **4** Chasseur, feldmarschmässig, 1800–1802. Er traget den habit-long und Uberknopfhosen. **5** Chasseurs einer Élite-Kompanie 1805–1806. Lant Dekret vom. 1. Oktober 1801 sind diese élite Einheiten aus den bestehenden 1. Kompanien des 1. Eskadron jedes Regiment errichtet worden. **6** Chasseurs einer Élite- unde einer Zentrums-Kompanie, 1805 im Interimsröcke (surtout), Überhosen und Stallmützen. **7** Chasseur, Stallanzug, 1805 – er worde normalerweise Holzschuhe tragen. **8** Offizier einer Élite-Kompanie 1805–1806. Die Pelmütze (colpack), ursprunglich fur diese Kompanie allein gedacht, wurde bald von den anderen Offizieren angenommen. **9** Offizier einer Zentrums-Kompanie, 1805–1806 mit dem Schako M1801 mit Turban. **10** Chasseur einer Élite-Kompanie, feldmarschmässig (zu Fuss), 1805–1806. Der Federbusch in dem Wachstuchüberzug beachten!

11 Chasseur einer Zentrums-Kompanie, feldmarschmässig 1805–1806. **12** Trompeter im '2. Anzug', 1806. **13** Colonel Baron Méda, 1. Chasseurs, 1807, in grosser Uniform. **14** (Links) Offizier in Interimsuniform mit Überrock und Hut, 1807. (Rechts) Oberoffizier, feldmarschmässig, 1807. **15** Chasseur, feldmarschmässig, 1807. Der Dolman beachten! **16** Chasseur, feldmarschmässig, 1809 mit dem 'Kinski-Rock' (eingeführt 1808) und den Dienstgradabzeichen eines brigadiers. **17** Chasseur einer Élite-Kompanie, 1813; er trägt, grob gesagt, die Uniform 1812 mit rot besetztem Schako. **18** Offizier in grosser Uniform, 1813. Die Uniform, ausser der Qualität und Zubehör, ähnelt sehr der der Mannschaftsuniform dieser Zeit. **19** Offizier, feldmarschmässig, 1813. Obwohl nicht in den Vorschriften von 1812 erwähnt, wurde die Pelzmütze von vielen immer noch getragen. Er trägt den 'redingote' Rock. **20** Chasseur einer Élite-Kompanie, feldmarschmässig, 1813, nach einer zeitgenossen Darstellung.

21 Chasseur in der inkompletten Uniformen und Ausrüstung, die für den Conscribierten von 1814 typisch waren. **22** Chasseur, 1. Regiment, 1815. Zu beginn der 'Hundert Tagen' trug das Regiment immer noch die Helme, die es während der 'Erste Restauration' bekommen hat. **23** Chasseur-Eskadron in Schlachtordnung: B=Brigadier, Bf=Brigadier-fourrier, M=Maréchal-des-logis. Mc=Maréchal-des-logis-chef, Am=Adjutant-major, Sl=Sous-Lieutenant, L=Lieutenant, C=Capitaine. **24** Erste Chasseur-Eskadron in 'colune serré' – Zeichenerklärung wie 23 oben. **25** Chasseur-Eskadron in 'colonne par divisions' – Zeichenerklärung wie 23 oben. **26** Chasseur-Eskadron in 'colonne par peletons' – Zeichenerklärung wie 23 oben. **27** Chasseur-Eskadron in 'Colonne von Vieren' – Zeichenerklärung wie 23 oben. **28** Dienstgradabzeichen zu Dolman und Pelisse: A=Brigadier, B=Brigadier-fourrier, C=Maréchal-des-logis, D=Maréchal-des-logis-chef, E=Adjutant-sous-officier, F=Sous-lieutenant, G=Lieutenant, H=Capitaine, I=Chef d'escadron, J=Major, K=Colonel. **29** Dienstgradabzeichen zu den habit-long, habit Kinski und habit-veste. Zeichenerklärung wie 28 oben.

30 Chasseur Kopfbedeckungen, 1790–1815. A1=Mirliton-mütze c. 1790 von vorne mit 'Flamme' losgebunden. A2=Mirliton von vorne, die schwarze Seite der Flamme ist sichtbar, wie im Dienstanzug. A3=Mirliton von Rechts mit der Flamme losgebunden. B1=Mirliton c. 1795 von vorne, mit dem Flamme losgebunden. B2=Mirliton mit der Flamme umgebunden, um die Abzeichenfarbe zu Zeigen, von Links gesehen. B3=Mirliton mit der Flamme in der Uhrzeigerichtung umgebunden, von Links gesehen. C1=Schako M1801 mit der Flamme ungebunden, von vorne gesehen. C2=Schako mit der Flamme in der Uhrzeigerichtung umgebunden, von vorne gesehen. C3=Schako mit der Flamme Linksumher gebunden. D=Schako M1806, getragen 1805–07. E=Schako M1806 getragen 1807–12. F=Colpack aus Bärenfell, 1805–14. G=Schako M1810. H=Schako M1812 für Élite-Kompanien. I=Schako M1810 für Offiziere. J=Schako M1812 ('Zylindrisch') für Mannschaften. K=Schako M1812 ('Zylindrisch') für Offiziere.

31 Waffen und Ausrüstungsstücke für Mannschaften. A=Husar-Säbel M1786. B=Chasseur-Säbel M1801. C=Leichte-Kavallerie-Säbel An XI. D=Gürtel mit Bayonettenscheide M1812. **32** Waffen und Ausrüstungsstücke für Offiziere. A=Säbel 'à l'Allemande'. B=Säbel 'à la hussarde'. C=Leichte-Kavallerie-Säbel An XI. D=Säbel 'à la chasseur' An XI. E=Gürtel M1812. F=Typische Cartouche und Bandolier. **33** Handfeuerwaffen und Zubehör. A=Husaren-Musketoon M1786. B=Bandoliere, Musketoon-Riemen und Patronentasche An IX. C=Musketoon An IX/XIII. D=Bandoliere, Musketoon-Riemen und Patronentasche M1812. E=Kavallerie-Pistole An XIII. **34** Bock und Zubehör des ungarischen Bocksttels. A=Seitenansicht. B=Ansicht von vorne. C=Ansicht von Hinten. D=Ansicht von oben. 1=Die Träger. 2=Der Sattelknopf. 3=Der Hinterzwiesel. 4=Der Sitz. 5=Der Gurt. 6=Der Vorderzeug. 7=Der Falsche Maringal. 8=Der Schwanzriemen. 9=Der Steigbügelriemen. 10=Die Pistolenhalfter. 11=Der Gewehr-Tiemen. 12=Der Musketoon-Stiefel. 13=Die Mantelriemen. **35** Satteln, Zaumzeug und Kopfstücke. A=Ungarisches Sattel und Schabracke für Regiments-Pferde. B=Ungarisches Kopfstück für Regiments-Pferde. C=Trense für Regiments-Pferde. D=Parade-Halfter für Kopfstück für Regiments-Pferde. E=Komplettes Zaumzeug und Zubehör für Offiziers-Pferde. F=Ungarischer Sattel in Leder für Offiziers-Pferde. G=Parade-Kopfstück für Pferde von Stabsoffizieren. H=Das Vorderzeug zu G oben. I=Ungarischer Sattel mit Leopardfell-Schabracke für Stabsoffiziere.

Farbtafeln

A1 Gemeiner, 5. Chasseurs, feldmarschmässig 1806. Er trägt den habit-long und den sogenannten Schako M1801. **A2** Trompeter, 1. Chasseurs, in grosser Uniform 1803 mit dem Dolman. Diese Jacke wurde sogar bis 1805 sorgfältig weitergetragen. **A3** Oberst, 5. Chasseurs, in grosser Uniform 1804. Dieses Regiment zog zuerst den colpack an.

B1 Brigadier, 1. Chasseurs, feldmarschmässig 1804–1805. **B2** Chef de Musique, 7. Chasseurs, in grosser Uniform, 1805–1806. **B3** Subaltern-offizier, 1. Chasseurs, Dienstanzug, 1806, in dem habit-long.

C1 Sous-officier, 10. Chasseurs, in grosser Uniform im 'Kinski-Rock'. **C2** Trompeter, 6. Chasseurs, in vollem Dienstanzug 1809. Eine typische Uniform für Mitglieder der 'tête du colonne'. **C3** Subaltern-offizier, 16. Chasseurs, in grosser Uniform 1809. Er trägt den habit-long und, wie üblich, ein hoch verzierten Leder-Bandolier, dass er selbst angeschafft hat.

D1 Gemeiner, 13. Chasseurs, feldmarschmässig, 1806. Ansicht von hinten mit habit-long. **D2** Trompeter, 7. Chasseurs, Dienstanzug 1810–1812. Die interessante Verzierung des Kinski-Rocks in gewechselten Farben beachten! **D3** Offizier, 4. Chasseurs, feldmarschmässig, 1809. Eine typische vereinfachte Feluniform.

E1 Gemeiner, 26. Chasseurs in grosser Uniform 1809–12. Der unbeliebte Schako M1806 wurde von verschiedenen Regimentern nach Geschmack umgebastelt und verziert. **E2** Trompeter, 24. Chasseurs, feldmarschmässig, 1809. Statt der üblichen grüne oder graue Überhosen, trägt er solche in himmelblauer Farbe. **E3** Stabsoffizier, 20. Chasseurs, in grosser Uniform, 1812. Die Parolis in der Regimentsfarbe auf dem Kinski-Rock beachten!

F1 Gemeiner, 7. Chasseurs, feldmarschmässig, 1811. Diese Uniform wurde in Spanien niedergeschrieben und durfte als typisch gelten. **F2** Trompeter, 11. Chasseurs in grosser Uniform, 1810. Als Ausnahme, erschien dieses ganze Regiment bis wenigstens September 1809 im habit-long. **F3** Stabs-offizier, 14. Chasseurs, Sommer-Ausgehanzug, 1810–1812.

G1 Gemeiner, 6. Chasseurs, Dienstanzug 1813–1814 mit dem Schako M1810. **G2** Trompeter, 12. Chasseurs, feldmarschmässig, 1810. Die ungewöhnliche Czapka Kopfbedeckung beachten! **G3** Subaltern-offizier, 8. Chasseurs in vorschriftsmässiger grosser Uniform 1813–1814, mit dem Schako M1812 und dem habit-veste.

H1 Gemeiner, 2. Chasseurs, feldmarschmässig 1813–1814 mit dem manteau-capote. **H2** Trompeter, 27. Chasseurs, grosser Uniform 1813–1814 in der kaiserlicher Livrée M1811 für Spielleute. **H3** Subaltern-offizier, 19. Chasseurs, feldmarschmässig, 1813–1814, in unvorschriftsmässigen colpack und dem neuen habit-veste.